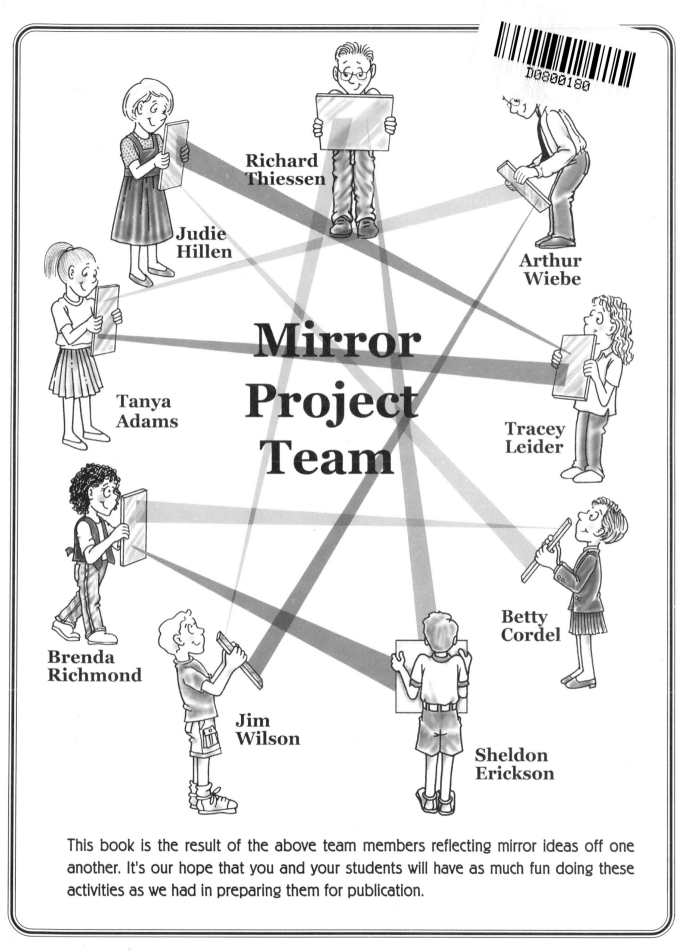

Mirror Project Team

Richard Thiessen

Judie Hillen

Arthur Wiebe

Tanya Adams

Tracey Leider

Brenda Richmond

Betty Cordel

Jim Wilson

Sheldon Erickson

This book is the result of the above team members reflecting mirror ideas off one another. It's our hope that you and your students will have as much fun doing these activities as we had in preparing them for publication.

This book contains materials developed by the AIMS Education Foundation. **AIMS** (**A**ctivities **I**ntegrating **M**athematics and **S**cience) began in 1981 with a grant from the National Science Foundation. The non-profit AIMS Education Foundation publishes hands-on instructional materials (books and the monthly magazine) that integrate curricular disciplines such as mathematics, science, language arts, and social studies. The Foundation sponsors a national program of professional development through which educators may gain both an understanding of the AIMS philosophy and expertise in teaching by integrated, hands-on methods.

Copyright © 2000 by the AIMS Education Foundation

All rights reserved. No part of this work may be reproduced or transmitted in any form or by any means—graphic, electronic, or mechanical, including photocopying, taping, or information storage/retrieval systems—without written permission of the publisher unless such copying is expressly permitted by federal copyright law. The following are exceptions to the foregoing statements:

- A person or school purchasing this AIMS publication is hereby granted permission to make up to 200 copies of any portion of it, provided these copies will be used for educational purposes and only at that school site.

- An educator providing a professional development workshop is granted permission to make up to 35 copies of student activity sheets or enough to use the lessons one time with one group.

Schools, school districts, and other non-profit educational agencies may purchase duplication rights for one or more books for use at one or more school sites. Contact the AIMS Education Foundation for specific, current information. Address inquiries to Duplication Rights, AIMS Education Foundation, P.O. Box 8120, Fresno, CA 93747-8120, toll-free (888)733-2467.

ISBN **1-881431-84-3**

Printed in the United States of America

Overview of Ray's Reflections

With *Ray's Reflections,* students learn the elementary geometry of points, lines, and angles by investigating the reflection of light from one or more plane mirrors.

The introductory activities invite students to observe images in the mirrors and to reflect light from the mirrors onto other objects. After they discover that they can redirect light by using mirrors, the following applications of this knowledge are made:

- They place mirrors along the darkened tunnels of "The Pharaoh's Chambers" in order to bring light into the innermost chamber of a pyramid.
- They make two simple "periscopes" that can be combined with those made by other students and direct light around corners.
- They play games of "pool" with light rays.

Students are now ready to explore several methods for determining that the image of an object seen in a mirror appears to be as far behind the mirror as the object is in front of the mirror and that the straight *line* connecting the object and its image is *perpendicular to* the mirror.

Several additional activities provide different ways for students to ascertain that the *angle* at which a light *ray* is reflected from a plane mirror equals the angle at which the ray strikes the mirror. This is the law of reflection for plane mirrors.

Students find that mirrors serve as a fascinating tool for exploring symmetry as they place a mirror inside or next to letters of the alphabet to find out which letters have one or more *lines of symmetry.* They then use this knowledge to write "secret" messages.

Finally, two plane mirrors hinged along an edge are used to create multiple reflections of both points and lines. Students delight in the kaleidoscope-like effects they can create with hinged mirrors.

All along the way, students discover that the science vocabulary and concepts used to describe plane mirror reflection "mirrors" that of the mathematical vocabulary and concepts used to describe geometric *points, lines* and *angles.*

Ray's Reflections truly does take students on an exciting integrated math/science journey.

 © 2000 AIMS Education Foundation

Ray's Reflections

The activities in *Ray's Reflections* are grouped by the mirror reflection concept emphasized in the activity. The first activity in each category is an introductory activity. Subsequent activities (in the same category) provide a different way to do, observe, and think about the same concept. Each category also emphasizes either the mathematical law of line symmetry or the scientific law of plane mirror reflection.

Introductory Activities

Reflection in a Single Mirror

What Does a Mirror Do?
Nose to Nose

Multiple Reflections from Several Mirrors

Catch a Ray
The Pharaoh's Chambers
Ray's Around the Corner
Pool Cues and Clues

Activities that Locate the Mirror Image

Put Your Finger on Ray
Reflections of Ray
Line of Sight
Put Your Finger on Ray, Again
Behind the Looking Glass

Activities that Trace the Light Path

Looking for Ray
Likely Reflections
Second Sight

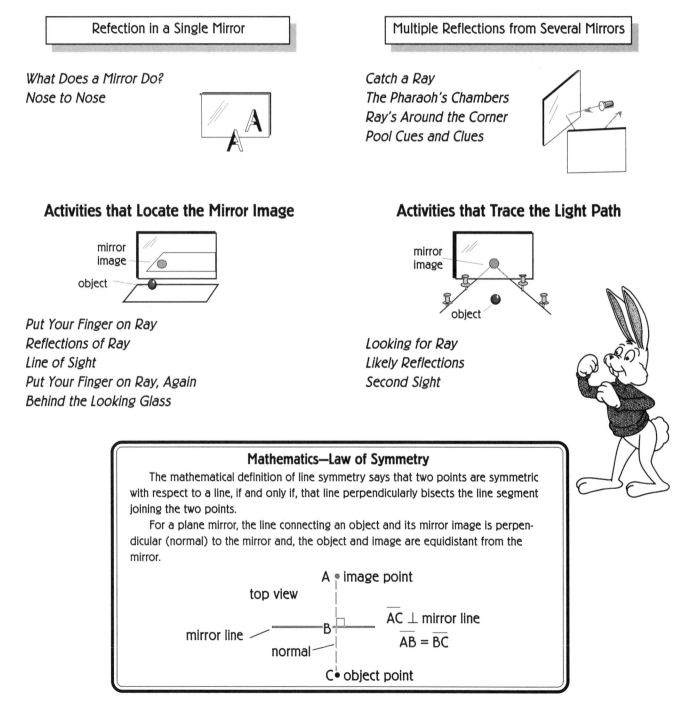

Mathematics—Law of Symmetry

The mathematical definition of line symmetry says that two points are symmetric with respect to a line, if and only if, that line perpendicularly bisects the line segment joining the two points.

For a plane mirror, the line connecting an object and its mirror image is perpendicular (normal) to the mirror and, the object and image are equidistant from the mirror.

top view

A • image point

mirror line

B

normal

C • object point

$\overline{AC} \perp$ mirror line

$\overline{AB} = \overline{BC}$

iv

© 2000 AIMS Education Foundation

Activities that Explore the Multiple Reflections Created in Two Facing Mirrors

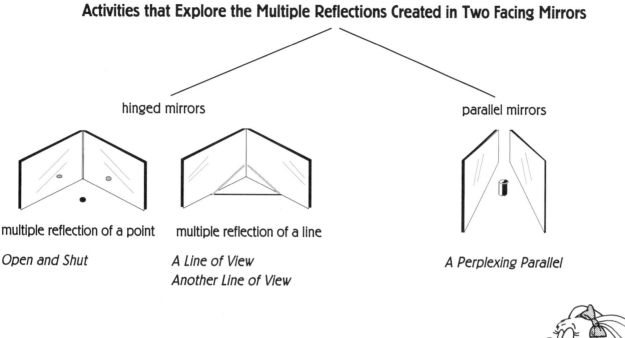

hinged mirrors

multiple reflection of a point

Open and Shut

multiple reflection of a line

A Line of View
Another Line of View

parallel mirrors

A Perplexing Parallel

Activities that Explore Line Symmetry

Hooray for Rabbit Ray!
Mirror Twins
A Hat Trick

The *Mirror Math* section lists the geometry concepts used in *Ray's Reflections* and correlates each concept to its science counterpart.

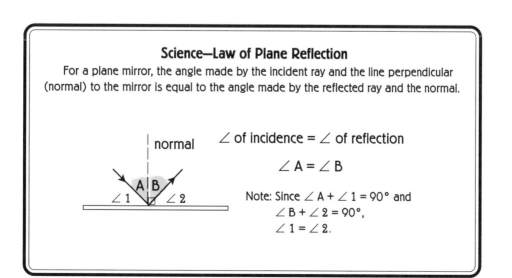

Science—Law of Plane Reflection

For a plane mirror, the angle made by the incident ray and the line perpendicular (normal) to the mirror is equal to the angle made by the reflected ray and the normal.

normal

$\angle 1$ $\angle 2$

$\angle$ of incidence = $\angle$ of reflection

$$\angle A = \angle B$$

Note: Since $\angle A + \angle 1 = 90°$ and
$\angle B + \angle 2 = 90°$,
$\angle 1 = \angle 2$.

Table of Contents

Drawing the Mirror Line for an Ordinary Mirror

In an ordinary mirror the reflective material is on the back of the mirror. The mirror line is therefore drawn at the back, not the front, of an ordinary mirror.

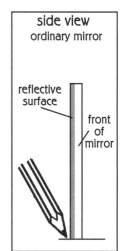

side view
ordinary mirror

reflective surface

front of mirror

1. The short horizontal line segment, $\overline{AB}$, is halfway between the longer vertical line segment, $\overline{CD}$.

2. Place the left end of an ordinary mirror on the dashed line. As you look into the mirror, move the mirror up and down the page, keeping the left end of the mirror on the dashed line, until the reflection of the circle at *D* matches the top line at *C*.

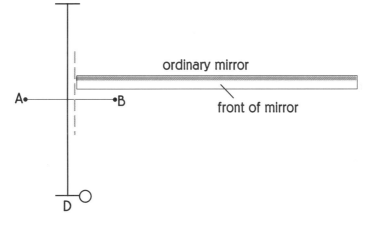

ordinary mirror

front of mirror

3. Make a mark at the back left edge of the mirror and the back right edge of the mirror. Remove the mirror and draw the straight line between the two marks. This indicates the mirror line.

pencil mark   mirror   pencil mark

4. Practice by drawing the mirror line for each of these segments. Use a millimeter ruler to check that the mirror line is halfway between $\overline{CD}$.

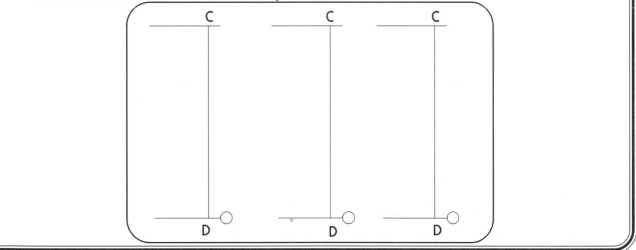

The Reflective Properties of an Ordinary Plane Mirror and a Transparent Plane Mirror

In an ordinary mirror, one surface of a transparent material is covered with a reflective material. This material reflects incident light back through the transparent material. Most of the light striking such a mirror is reflected off the rear surface of the mirror. The transparent material protects the reflective material.

In contrast, most of the light striking a transparent piece of colored plastic is reflected off its front surface. The Reflect/View, used in many of the activities contained in this book, is a red, transparent plastic mirror of this type.

To see one of the effects this difference causes, do the following test.

1. Place a Reflect/View along the horizontal dashed line. Find the image of the solid dot. Put the tip of your pencil on the solid dot. Mark the location of this image behind the Reflect/View .

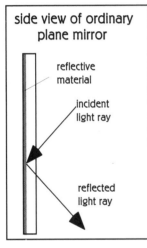

side view of ordinary plane mirror

reflective material

incident light ray

reflected light ray

2. Replace the Reflect/View with an ordinary mirror. Find the image of the solid dot. The image is clearly seen in the mirror. Now try to put the tip of your pencil on the image of the solid dot. Keeping your head steady and using both hands, raise the ordinary mirror straight up until you begin to see the pencil marked image behind the mirror. It appears that the image of the solid dot seen in the ordinary mirror is located at the same position as the image

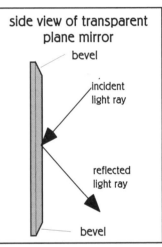

side view of transparent plane mirror

bevel

incident light ray

reflected light ray

bevel

marked when viewed through the Reflect/View. Therefore, one difference between using a transparent mirror like the Reflect/View and an ordinary mirror is that you can see behind a transparent mirror but not an ordinary mirror.

- -

●

 © 2000 AIMS Education Foundation

Drawing the Mirror Line for a Transparent Mirror

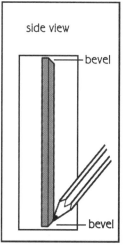

side view

bevel

bevel

1. The short horizontal line segment, $\overline{AB}$, is halfway between the longer vertical line segment, $\overline{CD}$.
2. Place the transparent mirror along the segment $\overline{AB}$ and adjust the mirror until the reflection of the circle matches the top line.
3. Carefully observe the position of the segment $\overline{AB}$. Does it touch the mirror?
4. Place your pencil under the bevel along the bottom edge of the mirror. Adjust the angle of your pencil so that you trace directly over the line. This is the "correct" angle for drawing a line that accurately represents the front surface, the mirror line, of a transparent mirror.
5. Practice by drawing the mirror line for each of these segments. Use a millimeter ruler to check that the mirror line is halfway between $\overline{CD}$.
6. Draw the mirror line for each of these segments. The mirror line must pass through the intersection of the crossed lines.

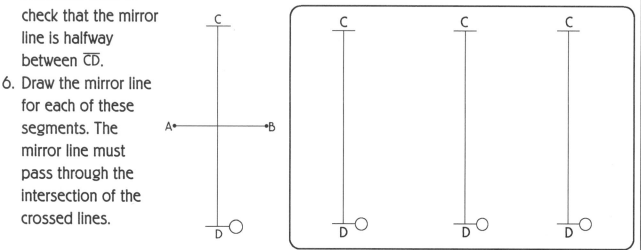

mirror line

Mirror Math

The study of the reflection of light from plane mirrors is an unusually rich example of the integration of mathematics and science. Much of the science vocabulary used in describing the behavior of light and its reflection from a plane mirror has a distinct similarity to the mathematical vocabulary used to describe geometric points, lines, and angles.

Both vocabularies provide students the language elements necessary to describe the observations and discoveries they will make as they study the interaction between light and a plane mirror.

To heighten this correlation, the appropriate language of science and mathematics will be developed side by side.

Light	Geometry

Point

Light is generally thought of as originating from a single point.

For example, think of a light bulb located at point A as a source of light.

Or the sun located at point B.

Line

Light travels in a straight line until it is reflected, refracted, or absorbed.

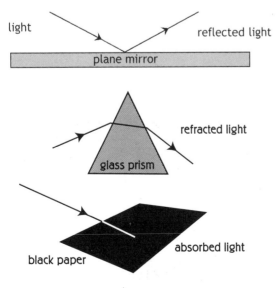

Point

A geometric point represents a single, exact location. A geometric point is represented by a small dot.

● geometric point

Uppercase letters are used to name points.

●A   point labeled A

Line

A straight line can always be drawn through any two points.

The arrows mean that the line extends indefinitely in the direction indicated by the arrows.

$\overleftrightarrow{AB}$ is the symbol for the line passing through the points A and B.

Line Segment

That portion of the line between and including the endpoints A and B is a line segment. $\overline{AB}$ is the symbol for the line segment.

x © 2000 AIMS Education Foundation

Mirror Math

Light	Geometry

Light

Line, continued
Ray

If a source of light is thought of as a point, then it is easy to describe the light given off by the source in terms of light rays.

For example, light rays explain the sharp edges of shadows like those seen in the phases of the moon.

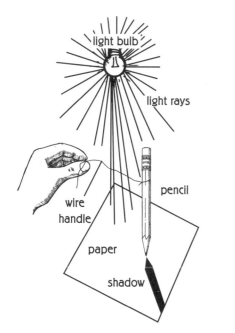

Geometry

Line, continued
Ray

A ray is that portion of a line starting at a point and going on forever in the direction indicated by the arrow.

$\overrightarrow{AB}$ is the symbol for the ray starting at point A, passing through point B, and continuing on forever in the direction indicated by the arrow.

The ray $\overrightarrow{BA}$ starts at point B and extends indefinitely through point A.

Any number of rays can originate from the same point.

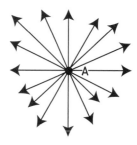

Enter Rabbit Ray

Rabbit Ray and Rabbit Raylynn Connect Light and Geometry

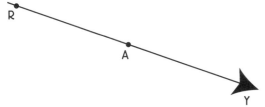

© 2000 AIMS Education Foundation

Mirror Math

Light | Geometry

Ray and Raylynn, representations of light rays, travel at high speed in a straight line until either strikes an object. We are going to study how Ray and Raylynn behave when either strikes a plane mirror.

A drawing of a geometric ray will be used to record Ray's or Raylynn's path. The ray records where Ray or Raylynn came from and where each went, the history of the journey, so to speak.

Lines other than rays will also be encountered in a study of reflection. The relationships between lines is important, both in plane reflection and in geometry.

Plane

A plane mirror is a flat mirror.

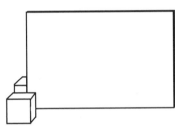

A plane mirror supported in a vertical position by blocks.

Plane

A geometric plane is thought of as a completely flat surface (no thickness) with no edges but extending on and on, without end, into space.

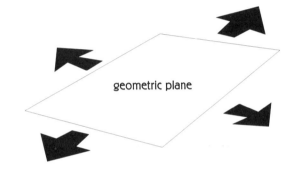

geometric plane

Intersecting Lines

The light rays from two different light sources in the same plane can cross each other, or intersect.

Intersecting Lines

Lines in the same plane either intersect or are parallel.

$\overleftrightarrow{AB}$ intersects $\overleftrightarrow{CD}$ at the point E.

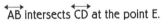

Perpendicular Lines

A line perpendicular to the baseline of a reflecting surface is called the normal line.

mirror standing vertically

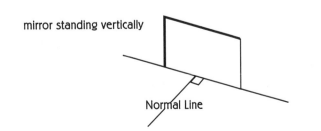

Normal Line

Perpendicular Lines

Line $\overleftrightarrow{AB}$ is perpendicular to line $\overleftrightarrow{CD}$ at the point E.

The symbol for perpendicular lines is ⊥.

$\overleftrightarrow{AB} \perp \overleftrightarrow{CD}$

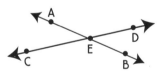

 © 2000 AIMS Education Foundation

Mirror Math

Light	Geometry

Parallel Lines

The light rays emitted by a laser are close to being parallel rays.

The light rays from distant sources are also close to being parallel.

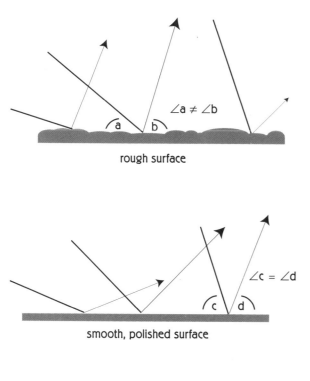

Angles

Light rays reflect off rough surfaces at angles different from the angles at which they strike the surface.

Light rays reflect off smooth, polished surfaces at angles equal to the angles at which they strike the surface.

rough surface

smooth, polished surface

Parallel Lines

Lines on a flat surface (in the same plane) that never intersect (have a point in common) are parallel lines.

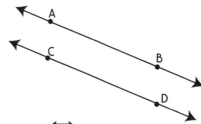

$\overleftrightarrow{AB}$ is parallel to $\overleftrightarrow{CD}$.
The symbol for parallel lines is ‖.

$$\overleftrightarrow{AB} \parallel \overleftrightarrow{CD}$$

Angles

The figure formed by two different rays starting from the same endpoint is called an angle. The symbol for angle is $\angle$.

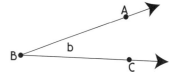

The ray $\overrightarrow{BA}$ is one side of the angle.

The ray $\overrightarrow{BC}$ is the other side of the angle.

The point B is the vertex of the angle.

The angle can be named in three ways:
1. By its sides and vertex, $\angle ABC$
2. By its vertex, $\angle B$
3. By the angle itself, $\angle b$

An angle with a measure less than 90° is an acute angle.

An angle with a measure greater than 90° but less than 180° is an obtuse angle.

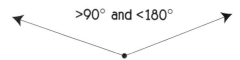

© 2000 AIMS Education Foundation

Mirror Math

Angles, continued

Perpendicular lines intersect each other at right angles.

$\overleftrightarrow{AB}$ is perpendicular to $\overleftrightarrow{CD}$.

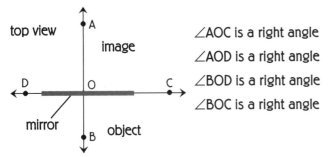

∠AOC is a right angle

∠AOD is a right angle

∠BOD is a right angle

∠BOC is a right angle

An angle with the vertex at the center of a circle and with sides along two radii is a central angle.

Two plane mirrors hinged at C form a central angle.

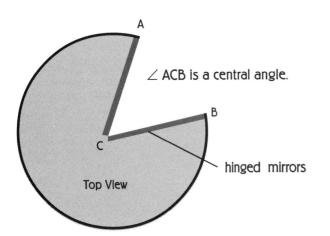

∠ ACB is a central angle.

Top View

hinged mirrors

Angles, continued

An angle with a measure of 90° is a right angle.

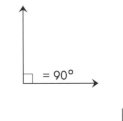

= 90°

The symbol for a right angle is

An angle with a measure of 180° is a straight angle.

= 180°

An angle with the vertex at the center of a circle and with sides along two radii is a central angle.

∠ ACB is a central angle.

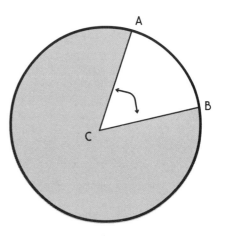

© 2000 AIMS Education Foundation

Mirror Math

Light | ## Geometry

Symmetry

Two points are symmetric with respect to a line if, and only if, the line perpendicularly bisects the line segment joining the two points.

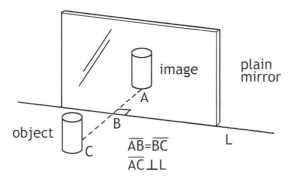

A geometric figure is symmetric with respect to a line if, and only if, every point on the figure on one side of the line is matched by a symmetrical point on the opposite side of the line of symmetry.

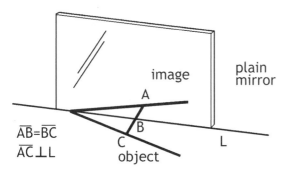

Symmetry

Two points are symmetric with respect to a line if, and only if, the line perpendicularly bisects the line segment joining the two points.

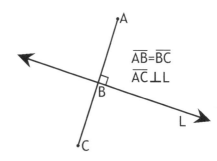

A geometric figure is symmetric with respect to a line if, and only if, every point on the figure on one side of the line is matched by a symmetrical point on the opposite side of the line of symmetry.

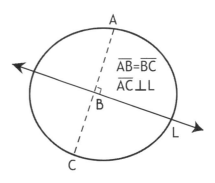

Mirror Math

Light	Geometry

Polygons

The image of a polygon can be created by reflecting a line segment in a hinged mirror.

line

Regular Polygons

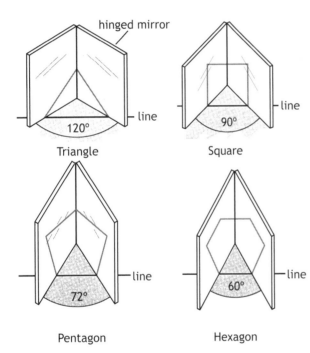

hinged mirror

line

120°
Triangle

line

90°
Square

line

72°
Pentagon

line

60°
Hexagon

Polygons

A polygon is a closed two-dimensional figure formed by the line segments that connect (without crossing) three or more points not in a straight line.

polygon

Regular Polygons

A regular polygon is a polygon in which all sides have equal lengths and all angles have equal measures.

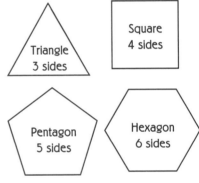

Triangle
3 sides

Square
4 sides

Pentagon
5 sides

Hexagon
6 sides

Convex Polygon

A convex polygon is a polygon in which each interior angle is less than 180°. Any straight line through a convex polygon intersects at most two sides. All the diagonals of a convex polygon are contained within the polygon.

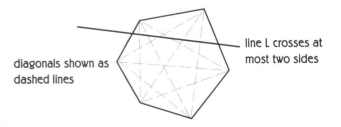

diagonals shown as dashed lines

line L crosses at most two sides

© 2000 AIMS Education Foundation

Mirror Math

Concave Polygon

Concave polygons can easily be observed in a hinged mirror by placing the vertex of the hinged mirror near, and to the side, of the reflected line.

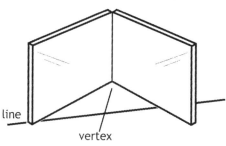

line

vertex

concave polygons

Concave Polygon

A concave polygon is a polygon in which at least one interior angle is more than 180°. Also, at least one straight line through a concave polygon intersects more than two sides. At least one diagonal is external to the polygon.

diagonals shown as dashed lines

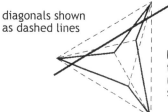

L

line L crosses the figure at more than two sides

Catch a Ray

Topic
Plane mirror reflection

Key Question
How can the direction a light beam is traveling be changed?

Focus
Students will use plane mirrors to catch a beam of light, redirect it into their classroom, and then redirect it into an empty cardboard box.

Guiding Documents
Project 2061 Benchmark
- *...Something can be "seen" when light waves emitted or reflected by it enter the eye...*

NRC Standards
- *Light travels in a straight line until it strikes an object. Light can be reflected by a mirror, refracted by a lens, or absorbed by the object.*
- *Light interacts with matter by transmission (including refraction), absorption, or scattering (including reflection). To see an object, light from the object—emitted by or scattered from it—must enter the eye.*

NCTM Standard 2000*
- *Recognize geometric ideas and relationships and apply them to other disciplines and to problems that arise in the classroom or in everyday life*

Math
Geometry and spatial sense
  angle
  mapping

Science
Physical science
  light
    plane reflection

Integrated Processes
Observing
Predicting
Identifying and controlling variables
Comparing and contrasting

Materials
For each group of three students:
  three plane mirrors
  one empty cardboard box

Background Information
This activity is designed to invite Rabbit Ray into your classroom. Rabbit Ray will be our tour guide as we travel through this book. Rabbit Ray has many of the characteristics of light: he moves fast, tends to travel in a straight line, changes direction when he strikes an object, and has "a story to tell." How light travels through lenses and bounces off mirrors is very predictable. That part of physical science concerned with predicting the future behavior of light or determining its past history is called *optics*. As Rabbit Ray says, "Ask me where I'm going, and I'll tell you where I've been."

In this activity each group of three students will attempt to *capture* Rabbit Ray and take him into their classroom. The first student will catch a beam of sunlight—Rabbit Ray—and direct it onto the mirror of the second student located near the door or window looking into the classroom. This second student will bounce the light beam onto the mirror of the third student whose job is to direct the beam into its assigned box.

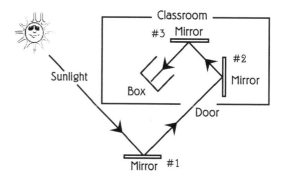

Students are asked to make of drawing of their solution to capturing Rabbit Ray and getting him into the box.

Management
1. Choose a sunny day for students to do this activity.
2. Organize students into groups of three.
3. If your classroom is too small, have students place their boxes in shaded playground locations.

Procedure

1. Explain the task to students.
2. Either assign student roles or let the students determine who is to catch the light beam outside of the classroom, who is to get the beam through a door or window into the classroom, and who is going to get the beam in the box.
3. Have each student team label a box and place it somewhere in the classroom.
4. Inform the students that you will verify whether or not each team has completed the task.
5. Distribute the student pages. Explain to students that not only are they to solve the problem of getting a beam of sunlight into the box but they will need to record their solution on their student page. Describe the set of symbols that appear at the bottom of their student sheet. Be sure they understand they don't need to locate every student's desk on their map.
6. Remind students to remember their location (indoors or outdoors) and the position of the mirrors so they can record their solutions on their maps.
7. Warn students **NOT TO REFLECT LIGHT INTO ANYONE'S EYES.**

Discussion

1. What did you think was easy about catching Ray? (Generally, it's easy for students to catch Ray and then establish the *approximate* positions and orientations of the remaining mirrors.)
2. What did you think was hard about getting Ray into the box? [It's hard to get Ray into the box and then **keep** Ray in the box since the slightest shift in position of any of the mirrors allows Ray to escape.]
3. What happens when you make even small variations in the *orientation* of your mirrors? [It makes large differences in the path the beam of light follows.] (If necessary, demonstrate this by reflecting the light from a flashlight (or other light source) off a mirror. At a distance of 25 feet, the center of a reflected light beam will move approximately five feet when the mirror is rotated through a five degree angle.)

Extension

Have four students attempt to get a beam of sunlight into a box. If successful, have five students, then six students, and so on, until it becomes too difficult to direct a beam of sunlight into a box. You might also *time* each attempt and then compare *number of mirrors* with *time*.

* Reprinted with permission from *Principles and Standards for School Mathematics,* 2000 by the National Council of Teachers of Mathematics. All rights reserved.

Catch a Ra

1. Make a drawing of your classroom. Use the symbols to locate the the doors and windows in your classroom.
2. Locate the position of your box on the map.
3. Indicate the direction of the sun.
4. Locate the position of each of the three mirrors.
5. Draw the path Rabbit Ray followed to enter your classroom and then enter the box.

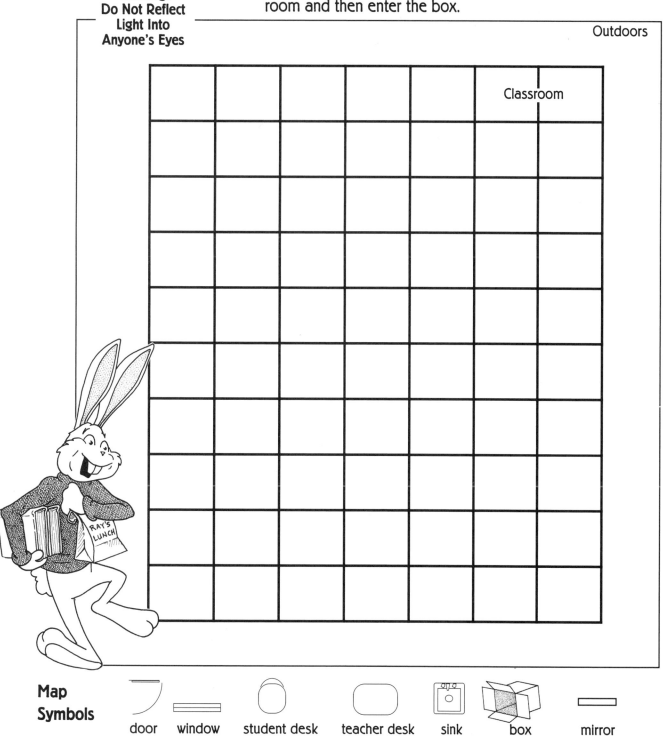

Warning! Do Not Reflect Light Into Anyone's Eyes

Outdoors

Classroom

Map Symbols

door window student desk teacher desk sink box mirror

What Does a Mirror Do?

What Does a Mirror Do?

Topic
Plane mirror reflection

Key Question
What does a mirror do?

Focus
Given a plane mirror, students will observe images in the mirror and reflect light from the mirror onto another object.

Guiding Documents
Project 2061 Benchmark
- *...Something can be "seen" when light waves emitted or reflected by it enter the eye...*

NRC Standards
- *Light travels in a straight line until it strikes an object. Light can be reflected by a mirror, refracted by a lens, or absorbed by the object.*
- *Light interacts with matter by transmission (including refraction), absorption, or scattering (including reflection). To see an object, light from the object—emitted by or scattered from it—must enter the eye.*

Science
Physical science
  light
    mirror image
    plane reflection

Integrated Processes
Observing
Predicting
Comparing and contrasting

Materials
For the class:
  table lamp with an unshaded bulb

For each student:
  plane mirror, approximately 3" by 4"

Background Information
This activity introduces students to the wonder and surprise encountered in a playful but thoughtful study of the interaction between light and a plane mirror. Many questions requiring answers will result from this activity. Be forewarned that it will take a *series of activities* to give students the experiences they will need in order to begin constructing explanations for what they observe. Keep students involved by encouraging their questions, asking *them* what *they* might do to answer their questions, and maintaining a comfortable and supportive environment for exploration.

The following are mileposts students will meet along the route of this activity. As they meet these mileposts, point them out to students.
- A mirror can redirect the path of light.
- Images can be seen in mirrors.
- Images in a mirror are alike and different from the objects themselves.
- Mirrors are "surfaces."
- Some surfaces make better mirrors than other surfaces.
- *Smoothness* is associated with mirrors.
- Some objects appear *symmetrical* when viewed in a mirror.

Management
1. Set the unshaded lamp in a spot visible to all students. Turn the light on before beginning the activity.
2. This activity needs your guiding hand. More questions will be raised than answered by doing this activity; this is often the first stage in learning something new.

Procedure
1. Ask the *Key Question.*
2. Allow the students time to explore with their mirrors.
3. After sufficient exploration time, instruct students to record on their activity page the things their mirrors can do.
4. Through discussion, develop a working definition of "mirror." For example, a mirror might be defined as any object in which one can recognize his/her own reflection.
5. Once a definition has been agreed on, instruct the students to find and record on their sheets objects that act like a mirror and objects that don't act like a mirror.
6. Have the students compare the objects that act like mirrors and describe how they are alike.
7. Ask the students to do the same with the objects they listed that don't act like mirrors.
8. Have the students decide what characteristic or characteristics an object must have in order to act like a mirror.
9. Direct the attention of the students to the title of their activity page. Ask them to study the "bottom line."
   Have students predict what will be seen in a mirror placed vertically on the line. [It can be seen in the mirror as *What Does a Mirror Do?*]

 © 2000 AIMS Education Foundation

10. Finally, let the students try to write their names below the line, upside down and backwards, so that it can be read in a mirror.

Discussion

1. What did you write in response to *Describe the things your mirror can do*? Collect student responses on the chalkboard or chart paper. The following are samples of actual student responses.

Describe the things your mirror can do.

reflect your image
send messages/signals
see what's behind you
to shave
to put on make-up
to brush your teeth
"doubles" things

Give students time to amend their activity sheets. They will quickly verify claims made by other students that they did not think of.

2. Inform students about any mirror property they failed to discover and add that property to the collection. For example, did anyone notice that the mirror appears to reverse "left" and "right"? Invite students to contribute examples of this reversal.

3. What objects act like a mirror? What objects don't act like a mirror? Again, record the responses. The following are actual student responses:

What objects act like a mirror?	What objects don't act like a mirror?
window	door
TV screen	desk
clock	paper
poster	skin
eyeglasses	T-shirt
overhead	chair
microwave door	chalkboard

4. How are the objects that act like a mirror alike? How are the objects that don't act like a mirror alike? The following are typical student responses:

Act like a mirror?	Don't act like a mirror?
cool	rough
smooth	soft
hard	dull
shiny	cool

Discuss some "exceptions to the rule." (For example, an ordinary rock does not make a good mirror, but what about the highly polished rocks made and sold by rock hounds or the natural, glass-like rock known as *obsidian*? Water is *soft* but its surface, when smooth, acts like a mirror.)

5. Have the students decide on the characteristics of an object that make it a good mirror. (*Smooth* and *shiny* are the characteristics for which it is difficult to find exceptions.) Challenge students to spend the next few days looking for objects that are good mirrors that are not smooth and shiny.

6. Use chart paper to collect the questions that are still unanswered. Don't worry if students don't generate a large number of questions. As they work more with mirrors, they will soon develop the comfort level needed for questions to arise. Students often won't ask questions if they think they'll have to provide immediate answers.

7. Historically, what are some things people used for mirrors? [shiny metal, water]

Extensions

1. The "upside down and backwards" method for mirror-writing names is easily extended to longer messages. Take a sheet of plain paper. Fold in half, top to bottom. Unfold and turn lengthwise. On the left side of the page, write your message as you normally would.

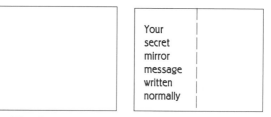

Flip the sheet of paper over. Use a dark marking pen to trace over the "backward" message seen through the paper. If necessary, place the sheet against a window to see the message.

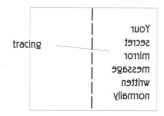

Fold the left side of the paper over the traced message and again trace the backward message. Open the paper, tear off and discard the right half. Turn the backwards message upside down and write "begin here" at the top of the paper. Glue the half-sheet to a piece of dark paper.

2. Does a mirror work in the dark? How would you design an experiment to determine whether or not a mirror does or does not work in a dark room?

What Does a Mirror Do?

What Does a Mirror Do?

Describe the things your mirror can do.

Look around the room.

What objects act like a mirror?

What objects don't act like a mirror?

Compare the items in the "act like a mirror" column. How are they alike?

Compare the items in the "don't act like a mirror" column. How are they alike?

What "characteristic" should an object have in order to be a good mirror?

The Pharaoh's Chambers

Topic
Plane mirror reflection

Key Question
The ancient Egyptians had a hieroglyphic for "mirror." How might the Egyptians have used mirrors to get light into their pyramids?

Focus
Students will orient a series of mirrors so that the combined reflections direct the incident light beam to a target.

Guiding Documents
Project 2061 Benchmark
- *…Something can be "seen" when light waves emitted or reflected by it enter the eye…*

NRC Standards
- *Light travels in a straight line unless it strikes an object. Light can be reflected by a mirror, refracted by a lens, or absorbed by the object.*
- *Light interacts with matter by transmission (including refraction), absorption, or scattering (including reflection). To see an object, light from the object—emitted by or scattered from it—must enter the eye.*

NCTM Standard 2000*
- *Recognize geometric ideas and relationships and apply them to other disciplines and to problems that arise in the classroom or in everyday life*

Math
Measurement
  length
  angle
Whole number operations

Science
Physical science
  light
    plane reflection

Integrated Processes
Observing
Collecting and recording data
Comparing and contrasting
Analyzing

Materials
For each group:
  four small mirrors with supports (see *Management 4*)
  flashlight
  metric ruler
  clear tape or glue sticks

Background Information
Egyptian Hieroglyphics

Hieroglyphic writing is the first of three kinds of script to evolve in Ancient Egypt. The pictorial hieroglyphic form developed into a cursive form called *hieratic*. By 700 B. C. a very rapid form of hieratic, called *demotic*, became the common writing of daily life. Hieroglyphic was used for "sacred" inscriptions chiseled or painted on temple walls, tomb walls, and public monuments.

In hieroglyphic writing only two types of signs are used. They are *ideograms* and *phonograms*.

Ideograms convey their meanings pictorially. This ideogram means *god* or *pharaoh*.

Phonograms are sound-signs that have sound-values used for spelling. The phonogram, pronounced *m* (em) means 1. in; 2. by means of, with; or 3. from, out of.

Hieroglyphic writing consists of vertical columns or horizontal lines. The direction of the writing is from top to bottom for columns and left to right or right to left for lines. The left to right or right to left direction of linear hieroglyphics is determined by the direction the ideograms are facing. For example, if the ideogram for "god" is facing to the left, then the text is read left to right.

Egyptian hieroglyphics expressed numbers using a *simple grouping system.* In such a system a number *b* is selected to be the number base and symbols for 1, *b*, b^2, b^3, b^4, and so on are used. A number is then expressed in this system by using the base symbols *additively*. For example, a vertical stroke represents 1, a yoke represents 10, a coil of rope is 100, and a lotus flower is the symbol for 1000. In the Egyptian system the number 1322 would be represented as

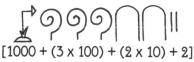

[1000 + (3 x 100) + (2 x 10) + 2]

Hieroglyphic symbols are included in this activity for their historical value.

The tombs and chambers inside pyramids were often decorated with intricate and brightly colored hieroglyphic inscriptions.

It's a matter of speculation as to how the workers and artists were able to see clearly enough to work in these tombs and chambers. The absence of soot marks from torches indicates these workers were able to get light inside even though they were deep inside the pyramid. One theory is that they used highly polished metal sheets to direct light into the pyramid and then used other mirrors to redirect it into the various chambers.

 © 2000 AIMS Education Foundation

This is the hieroglyphic ideogram for copper or bronze.

This is the hieroglyphic for mirror.

The fact that the ideogram for a metal that can be highly polished is part of the ideogram for *mirror* is an indication that the ancient Egyptians may have used highly polished sheets of metal as mirrors.

Multiple reflections

Any mirror reflects only a percentage of the light striking its reflective surface. The *efficiency* of a mirror can be measured by the percentage of incident light the mirror reflects. For example, a mirror that reflects 66% of the light striking it has an efficiency of 0.66. A perfect mirror would have an efficiency of 1.0.

Assume a mirror reflects 50% of the light striking it—an efficiency of 0.5. If light is reflected off one mirror onto another mirror of the same efficiency, then the percentage of the incident light beam reflected off the second mirror is 0.25, or 0.5 x 0.5.

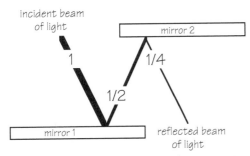

If each mirror in a chain of mirrors has the same efficiency, then total efficiency of the system is given by the mathematical equation, $E_{total} = E^n$, where n is the number of mirrors in the chain. For example, for a 50% efficient mirror and three reflections, $E_{total} = E^n$, $E_{total} = (0.5)^3$, $E_{total} = 0.125\%$ which is approximately 13% of the total.

In this activity students will find that the intensity of the light beam they eventually direct into the Pharaoh's chamber is relatively strong due to the high efficiency of the silvered mirrors they are using.

Management

1. This activity takes two class periods to complete. *Part One: The Pharaoh's Outer Chamber* gives the students the opportunity to solve a simple multiple-reflection problem. *Part Two: The Pharaoh's Inner Chambers* increases the number of reflections required to solve the problem.

2. The maps for both *Part One* and *Part Two* of this activity can be taped or glued together.

3. Rectangular mirrors, 6 cm by 4 cm or smaller, work best with this activity.

4. Each mirror needs to be supported so that it is stable in a vertical position. Binder clips or small wooden blocks work well as supports.

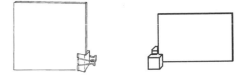

5. To familiarize yourself with its problem-solving elements, do the activity before presenting it to students.

6. Discuss how the pyramid cross-sectional maps and mirrors *model* what might have actually happened in the real pyramids when they were constructed. In the real pyramid, the polished metal mirrors would have to fit in the corridors whereas, in the model, the mirrors may not actually fit in the corridors.

7. Turn the lights off in the classroom to increase the apparent brightness of the reflected light beams.

Procedure

Part One

1. Distribute *The Pharaoh's Outer Chamber* map and a *Tunnel and Target Page* to each group. Instruct each group to cut and carefully tape or glue the two pages together to make a single map.

2. Have them use their metric rulers and pencils to draw straight lines between the points labeled *A* and *B*, *B* and *C*, and *C* and *D*. Tell them this is the path the beam of light should follow.

3. Have them cut out a tunnel piece one section long and tape it between the points *C* and *D*. Tape another single tunnel section between points *B* and *C*.

4. Give each group two mirrors.

5. Instruct them to cut out and tape the target piece, facing the light beam, at the point labeled *D*.

6. Instruct the students to place the flashlight at the point labeled *A* and direct the beam towards the point labeled *B*.

7. Have the students stand a mirror *on* the point labeled *B* and direct the light towards the point labeled *C*. Urge students to stand the eraser end of their pencils at point *C* to help direct the light beam.

8. Again, have the students stand a mirror at *C*, and reflect the beam coming from *B* towards the *Pharaoh's Outer Chamber,* striking the target at the point labeled *D*.

9. Once they have the mirrors aligned with the light striking the target, instruct them to mark the location of each mirror by marking along the bottom of each mirror.

10. Distribute the *Hieroglyphic Numbers* page. Explain the hieroglyphic example that appears on the student page. Inform the students that they will have to "look around," as archeologists do, to translate the hieroglyphics.

 © 2000 AIMS Education Foundation

Part Two
1. Distribute the four-page *The Pharaoh's Inner Chambers* map to each group. Instruct each group to cut and carefully tape or glue the upper-left page to the upper-right page and to carefully trim along the bottom lines.

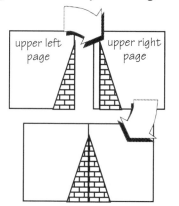

2. Instruct each group to cut and carefully tape or glue the lower-left page to the lower-right page.

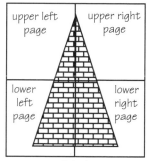

3. Now direct them to cut and carefully tape or glue the upper-half of the map to the lower-half to complete the map.

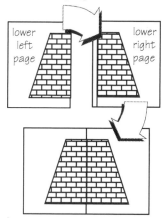

completed map

4. Distribute two *Tunnel and Target Pages* to each group. Instruct them to glue or tape one or more tunnel sections between each of the chambers.
5. Give each group four mirrors.
6. Have them use their metric rulers and pencils to draw straight lines between the points labeled *A* and *B*, *B* and *C*, *C* and *D*, *D* and *E*, and *E* and *F*. Tell them this is the path the beam of light should follow.

7. Instruct them to cut out and tape the target piece, facing the light beam at the point labeled *D*.
8. Instruct the students to place the flashlight at the point labeled *A* and direct the beam towards the point labeled *B*.
9. Have the students stand a mirror *near* the point labeled *B* and direct the light towards the point labeled *C*.
10. Again, have the students stand a mirror at *C*, and reflect the beam coming from *B* towards the *Pharaoh's Outer Chamber* at point *D*.
11. Tell them to direct the light beam off a mirror in the *Pharaoh's Outer Chamber* towards the *Pharaoh's Middle Chamber* at point *E*.
12. Now have them direct the beam from the Middle Chamber on into the Pharaoh's Chamber at point *F*.
13. Once they have the mirrors aligned with the light striking the target, instruct them to mark the location of each mirror by marking their paper along the bottom edge of each mirror.
14. Challenge the students to translate the panel of hieroglyphics displayed on the map. Again, inform them that they will have to "look around," as archeologists do, to translate the hieroglyphics.

Discussion
Part One
1. What's the relationship of the mirrors to each other? [The mirrors are approximately parallel.]
2. What's the relationship between each mirror and the angle at which the light strikes the mirror (angle of incidence) and the angle at which the light leaves the mirror (the angle of reflection)? [At each mirror, the angle of incidence is approximately equal the angle of reflection.]
3. Describe the brightness of the light beam reaching the chamber.
4. What is the translation of the scroll describing the Pharaoh's wealth on the *Hieroglyphic Numbers* page? (Students will need to use the hieroglyphics that appear on *The Pharaoh's Outer Chamber* map.)

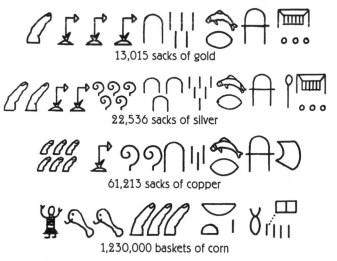

13,015 sacks of gold

22,536 sacks of silver

61,213 sacks of copper

1,230,000 baskets of corn

5. Contrast writing numbers using the multiplicative grouping system of the Egyptians with the modern place value, powers of ten system.

6. Do any hieroglyphic symbols represent more than one letter of the English alphabet? Explain. [Yes, the quail chick, door bolt, basket, and reed flower symbols each represent more than one English letter.]

Part Two

1. What's the relationship among each mirror, the angle at which light strikes the mirror, and the angle at which light is reflected off the mirror.

2. Describe the brightness of the light beam reaching the Pharaoh's Chamber.

3. What problems did you have translating the hieroglyphic message? Do you think your translation is accurate? Explain. (Students will be able to find a translation for most of the hieroglyphics in the message.)

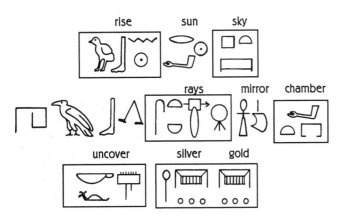

[The block of hieroglyphics pictured below is not translated anywhere in the materials.

Therefore, this block of hieroglyphics has to be translated *from the context* of the situation and the rest of the message. The hieroglyphic block could be translated as *send* or *direct*.

A good translation of the whole message is, *When the sun rises in the sky, send (or direct) rays off a mirror into the chamber to uncover silver and gold.*]

Extensions

1. Distribute the *Hieroglyphic Alphabet* and *Cartouche Frame* pages. Instruct students to follow the instructions and make a cartouche of their first name.

2. Have students integrate this activity with a social studies or history report about the ancient Egyptians.
   Potential topics:
   - *The Purpose of the Pyramids*
   - *How the Pyramids Were Constructed*
   - *Egyptian Mathematics*
   - *The Book of the Dead*
   - *Lord Carnarvon*
   - *Howard Carter*
   - *Valley of the Kings*
   - *Tutankhamun*
   - *Mummification*

* Reprinted with permission from *Principles and Standards for School Mathematics,* 2000 by the National Council of Teachers of Mathematics. All rights reserved.

 © 2000 AIMS Education Foundation

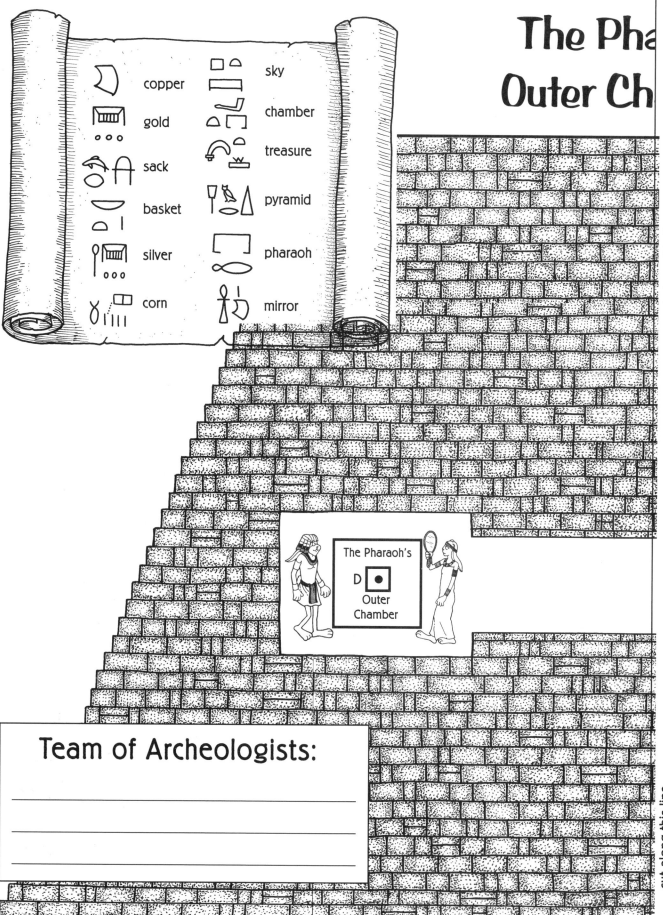

copper

gold

sack

basket

silver

corn

sky

chamber

treasure

pyramid

pharaoh

mirror

The Pha
Outer Ch

The Pharaoh's

D □•

Outer Chamber

Team of Archeologists:

_____

_____

_____

cut along this line

cut along this line

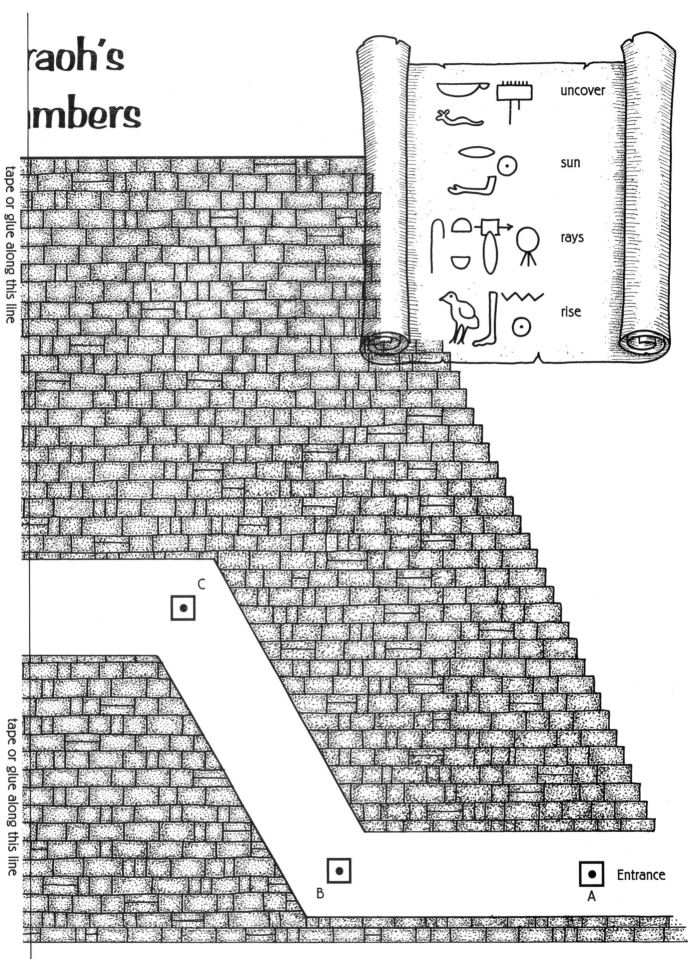

uncover

sun

rays

rise

C

B

Entrance
A

tape or glue along this line

tape or glue along this line

12

© 2000 AIMS Education Foundation

1 section   2 sections   3 sections

Tunnel and Target Page

Tunnel Instructions:

1. To make tunnels for the reflected light to pass through, cut and fold each tunnel piece as shown in the following diagram. Cut along the dark section lines to make shorter tunnels.

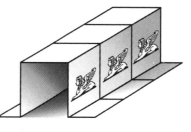

2. Tape or glue the tunnels along the tunnel lines on the map.

Target Instructions:

1. To make a target for adjusting the light beam reflected off a mirror, cut out the figure and fold along the dashed line.

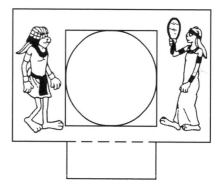

2. Place the figure at the end of the light path you're adjusting. Adjust your mirror(s) until the target is as bright as possible.

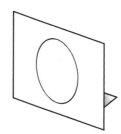

© 2000 AIMS Education Foundation

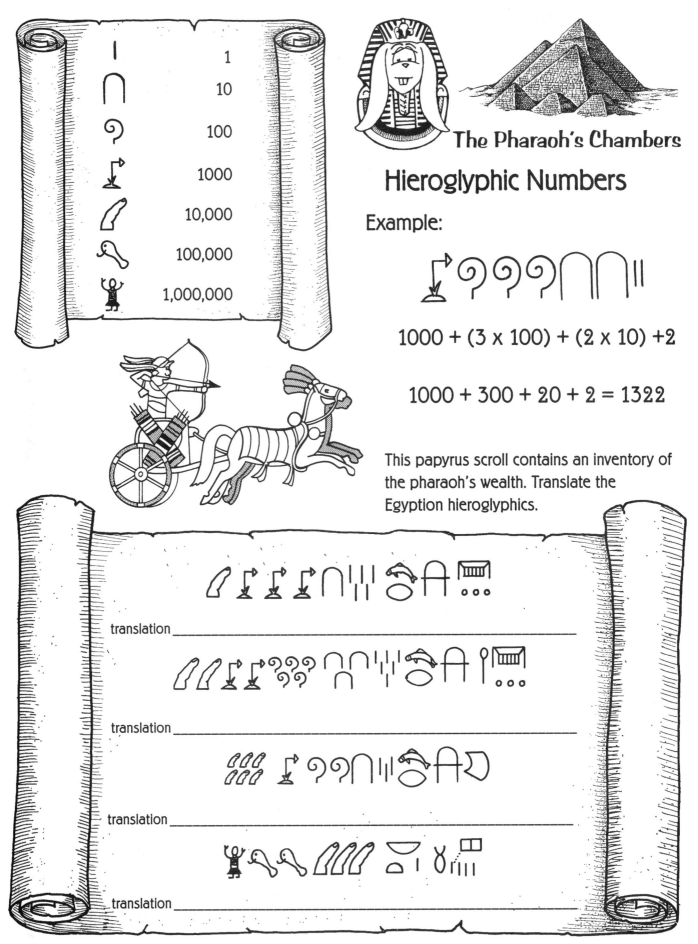

The Pharaoh's Chambers
Hieroglyphic Numbers

Example:

$1000 + (3 \times 100) + (2 \times 10) + 2$

$1000 + 300 + 20 + 2 = 1322$

This papyrus scroll contains an inventory of the pharaoh's wealth. Translate the Egyption hieroglyphics.

translation _____

translation _____

translation _____

translation _____

The Pharaoh's Inner Chambers

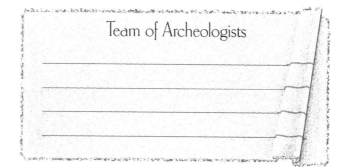

Team of Archeologists

A Challenge to Expert Egyptologists:
Use your knowledge of Egyptian hieroglyphics to translate this panel of hieroglyphics found on the outside of the pyramid.

cut along this line

upper right

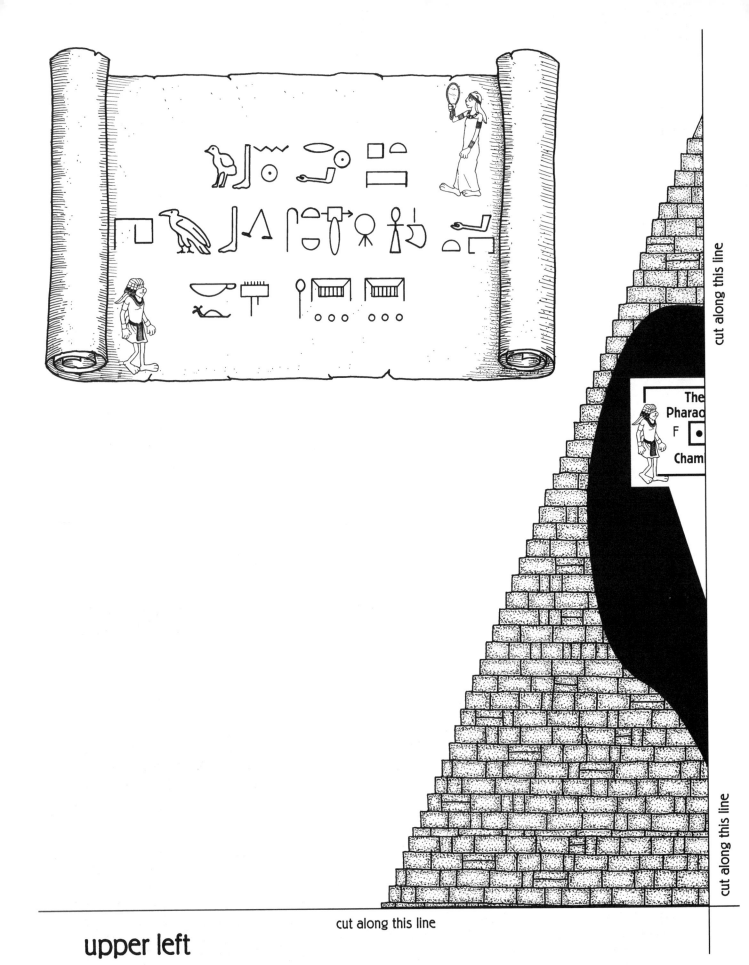

cut along this line

The
Pharao
F •
Cham

cut along this line

cut along this line

upper left

The Pharaoh's Chambers

cut along this line

Tape or glue along this line

Translation:

The Pharaoh's

D ▣

Outer Chamber

cut along this line

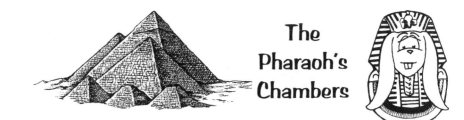

The Pharaoh's Chambers

lower right

tape or glue along this line

tape or glue along this line

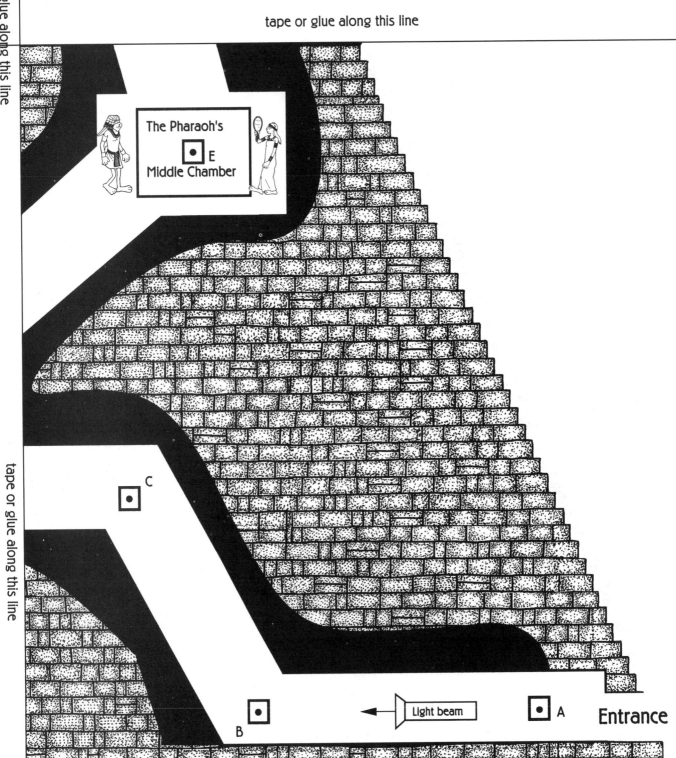

The Pharaoh's
■● E
Middle Chamber

● C

● B

Light beam

● A

Entrance

        © 2000 AIMS Education Foundation

The Pharaoh's Chambers

Hieroglyphic Alphabet

Every pharaoh and queen of ancient Egypt had a cartouche (kartoosh), a hieroglyphic nameplate or seal.

The cartouches for the names Casey and Rabbit Ray are shown here.

Design a cartouche of your first name.

Cut out and glue the hieroglyphics of your name in one of the frames. If your name has double letters get the extra letter(s) from a classmate.

Use colored pencils or felt-tip pens to add color to your cartouche.

Glue your completed cartouche to cardboard.

Wear your cartouche around your neck on a piece of string or yarn just like the pharaohs and queens of old.

vulture	foot	door bolt	hand	reed flower	horned viper	jar stand	courtyard	reed flower
A	B	C	D	E	F	G	H	I

snake	basket	lion	owl	water	rope	stool	hill	mouth
J	K	L	M	N	O	P	Q	R

hooked stick	bread loaf	Quail chick	horned viper	Quail chick	basket	2 reeds	door bolt	
S	T	U	V	W	X	Y	Z	

     © 2000 AIMS Education Foundation

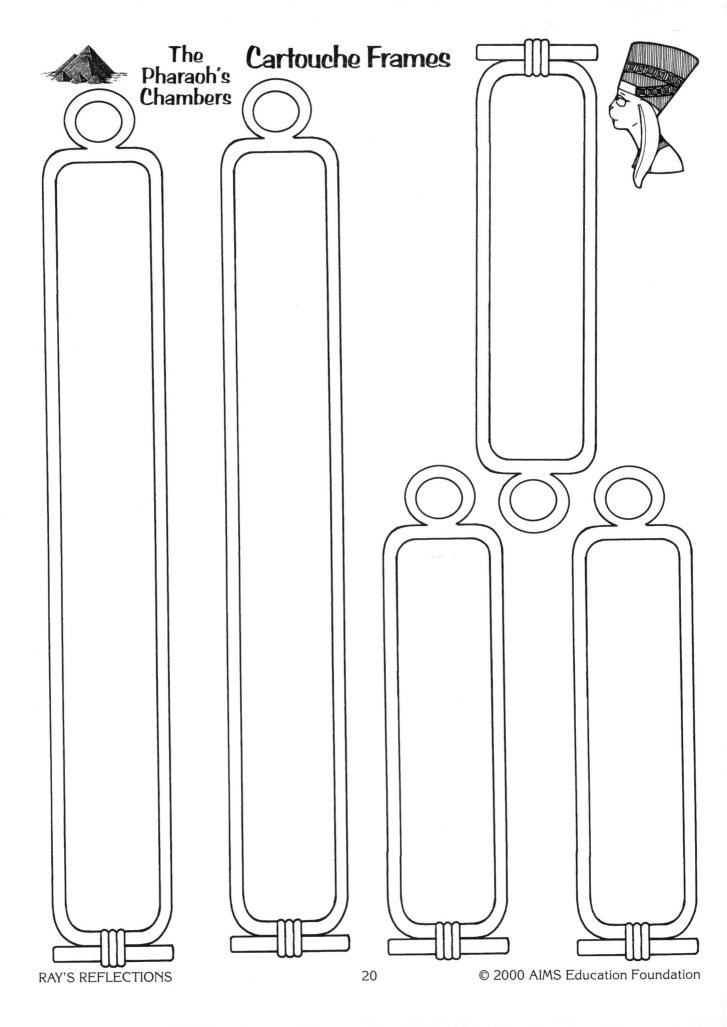

Cartouche Frames

© 2000 AIMS Education Foundation

Around the Corner

Topic
Plane mirror reflection

Key Question
How can two mirrors be placed so you can see an object placed around a corner?

Focus
Students will determine the placement of two mirrors so that they reflect light around two corners and make visible an object which before was hidden to the viewer.

Guiding Documents
Project 2061 Benchmark
- *…Something can be "seen" when light waves emitted or reflected by it enter the eye…*

NRC Standards
- *Light travels in a straight line until it strikes an object. Light can be reflected by a mirror, refracted by a lens, or absorbed by the object.*
- *Light interacts with matter by transmission (including refraction), absorption, or scattering (including reflection). To see an object, light from the object—emitted by or scattered from it—must enter the eye.*

NCTM Standards 2000*
- *Recognize geometric ideas and relationships and apply them to other disciplines and to problems that arise in the classroom or in everyday life*
- *Understand relationships among the angles, side lengths, perimeters, areas, and volumes of similar objects*

Math
Geometry and spatial sense
Measurement
 angle
Estimating

Science
Physical science
 light
 plane reflection

Integrated Processes
Observing
Predicting
Inferring

Materials
For each pair of students:
 one *Rabbit Ray Stand-up Figure*
 two plane mirrors
 scissors
 transparent tape or glue sticks

Background Information
Light is a form of energy. It travels in a straight line until it is reflected, refracted, diffracted, or absorbed. In a vacuum, light travels at the phenomenal speed of 186,000 miles per second. A geometrical *ray* is often the mathematical model scientists use to think about the behavior of light.

Almost everyone has an intuitive understanding of the law of plane reflection. Bouncing a rubber ball off a flat wall, reflecting a basketball off the backboard and into the net, and shooting balls off cushions in a game of pool are just a few of the everyday activities that make use of the law of plane reflection. Playing games such as these soon leads to an intuitive understanding that the angle at which an object strikes a flat surface—*angle of incidence*—equals the angle at which the object is reflected from the surface—*angle of reflection*. In science books, these angles are measured from a line perpendicular to the reflecting surface. This line is called the *normal*.

Regular Reflection

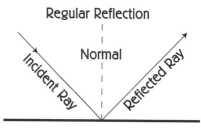

Angle measure, especially using a protractor, is often difficult for students to master. In this activity, students will continue to build on their intuitive understanding of how mirrors reflect images rather than to focus on the measurement of angles. The students will build two tunnel structures—one zigzagged and the other in a U-shape—in which they are challenged to position mirrors in order to see the character Rabbit Ray at the opposite end of the tunnel. (The character Rabbit Ray helps students build their conceptual understanding of the behavior of light. Rabbit Ray starts somewhere and travels, at high speed, in a straight line until, in this case, he is reflected off a mirror.) By angling the mirrors, students will discover that they can redirect

 © 2000 AIMS Education Foundation

the path of light, actually making the light rays turn corners. Our ability to direct a beam of light along a path of our choosing is used in such devices as cameras, telescopes, microscopes, and periscopes.

Management
1. Pair the students.
2. This activity can be divided into two parts. The first part is devoted to constructing the *Zigzag* and *U-Turn* pieces and solving each problem. The second part, which is optional and found in *Extensions 2,* provides students the time needed to explore combining the zigzagged and U-turn tunnels.

Procedure
1. Distribute student pages for the *Zigzag* shape and *The Tunnel Tubes.* One *Long Tunnel Tube* and two *Short Tunnel Tubes* are required.
2. Have students cut along the indicated line and glue or tape the two sheets together.
3. Show the students how to cut, roll, and tape or glue the *Tunnel Tubes.* Point out that the two shorter tubes have to be trimmed by cutting along the indicated lines. Instruct them to glue or tape the *Tunnel Tubes* to the *Zigzag* base.

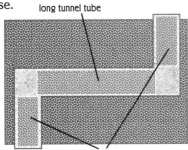

long tunnel tube

short tunnel tubes

4. Distribute the *Rabbit Ray Stand-up Figures.*
5. Direct the students to place a Rabbit Ray figure at the indicated position and one mirror at each indicated position.

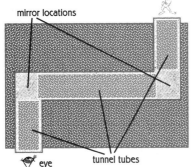

mirror locations

eye

tunnel tubes

6. Challenge them to adjust the positions of their mirrors so that Rabbit Ray can be seen "around the corners."
7. Once students have seen Rabbit Ray, have them use their pencils to trace the positions of the mirrors.
8. Have them follow the same procedure for the *U-Turn.*

Discussion
1. What did you have to do in order to see Rabbit Ray?
2. Did anyone discover an easy way to align your mirrors? [The reflection of a tunnel tube can be aligned to the actual tunnel tube. This guarantees that the reflected light is traveling straight down the tube.]
3. Describe the mirror position lines you drew. [They are angled across the mirror location areas.] What would happen if you positioned the mirrors parallel to either side of the tunnel? [You couldn't see Rabbit Ray.] Why? [His image would not be reflected in the mirror because it would not strike the mirror.]
4. Would you be able to see Rabbit Ray if you used only one mirror? Explain. [No, you have to redirect the light rays twice because there are two corners to each tunnel.]
5. Is the light path reversible? That is, can the positions of the "eye" and "object" be reversed? Explain. [The path is reversible. I can look through either end of the tunnel and see Rabbit Ray at the other end.]
6. Imagine you are Rabbit Ray. What would you see at the other end of the tunnel? (Have each pair of students actually remove the Rabbit Ray figure and position one person at each end of the tunnel.) [I would see the eye of my partner.]

Extensions
1. Hold the *Zigzag* in a vertical position and it becomes obvious that this shape is really a periscope. Encourage students to design and build their own periscopes from cardboard tubes or other suitable materials.

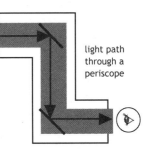

light path through a periscope

2. Each student pair will end the activity with two constructions, the *Zigzag* and the *U-Turn.* Each construction is modular and will connect to the other construction. Provide extra mirrors and encourage students to "chain" their constructions together. For example, the two constructions can be connected as shown in the diagram.

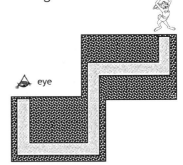

eye

3. Challenge students to team together and chain their four constructions together. This diagram shows one way two student pairs could chain their four constructions together.

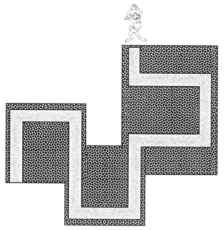

4. Encourage students to do research projects about how cameras, telescopes, microscopes, and periscopes bend light paths to their purposes.

5. Ray wants to be able to see Raylynn coming through the *Zigzag* tubes but doesn't want Raylynn to be able to see him. How can he do this? [Ray can build a wall with a small hole in it. Ray will be able to see Raylynn, but Raylynn won't be able to see Ray. Try it.]

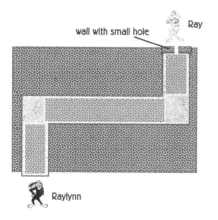

*   Reprinted with permission from *Principles and Standards for School Mathematics,* 2000 by the National Council of Teachers of Mathematics. All rights reserved.

Rabbit Ray Stand-up Figures

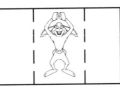

Instructions

1. Cut out the figure of Rabbit Ray along the solid lines.

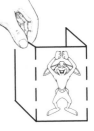

2. Fold the sides of the figure along the dashed lines.

3. The figure can be easily positioned by grasping it along the folded edge.

Copy onto card stock.

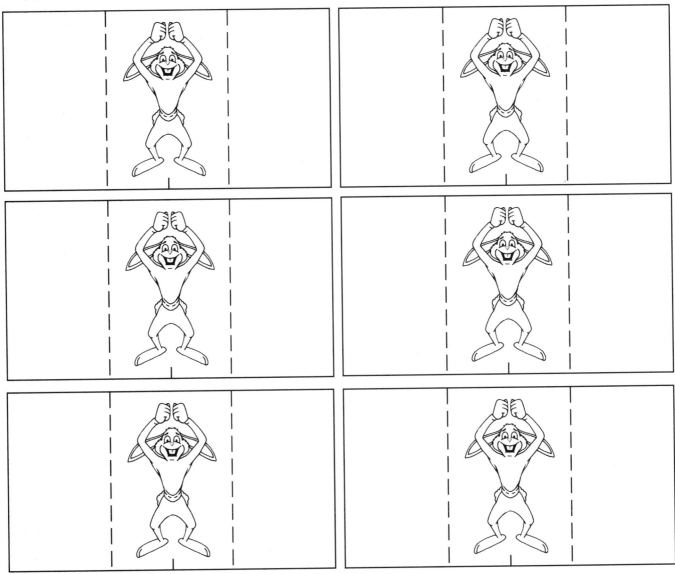

Long Tunnel Tube

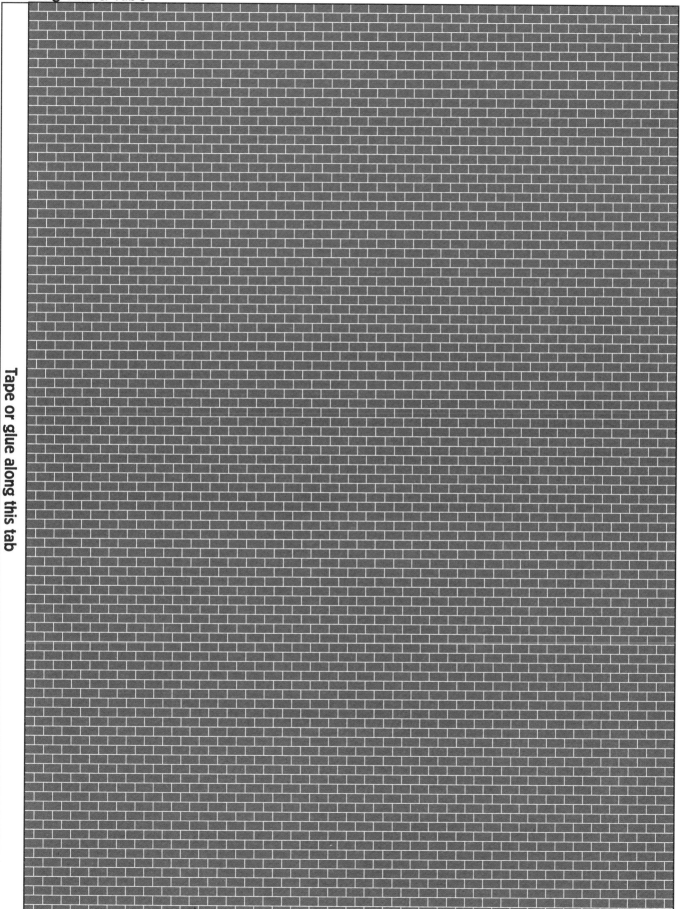

Tape or glue along this tab

                    © 2000 AIMS Education Foundation

Short Tunnel Tubes

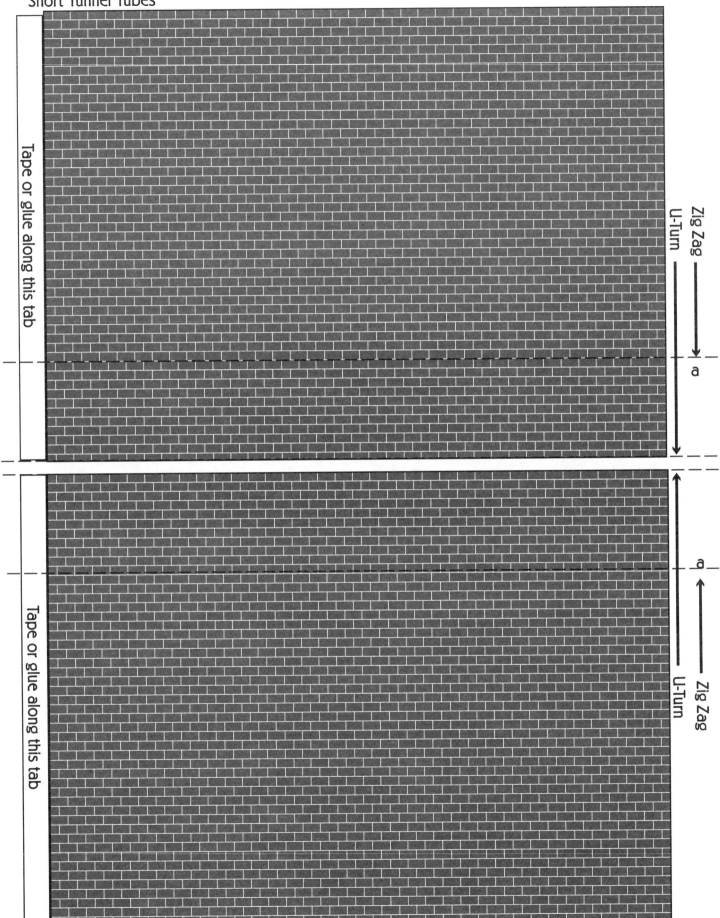

Mirror
Location 2

Cut along this line

Place Short Tunnel Tube here

27

© 2000 AIMS Education Foundation

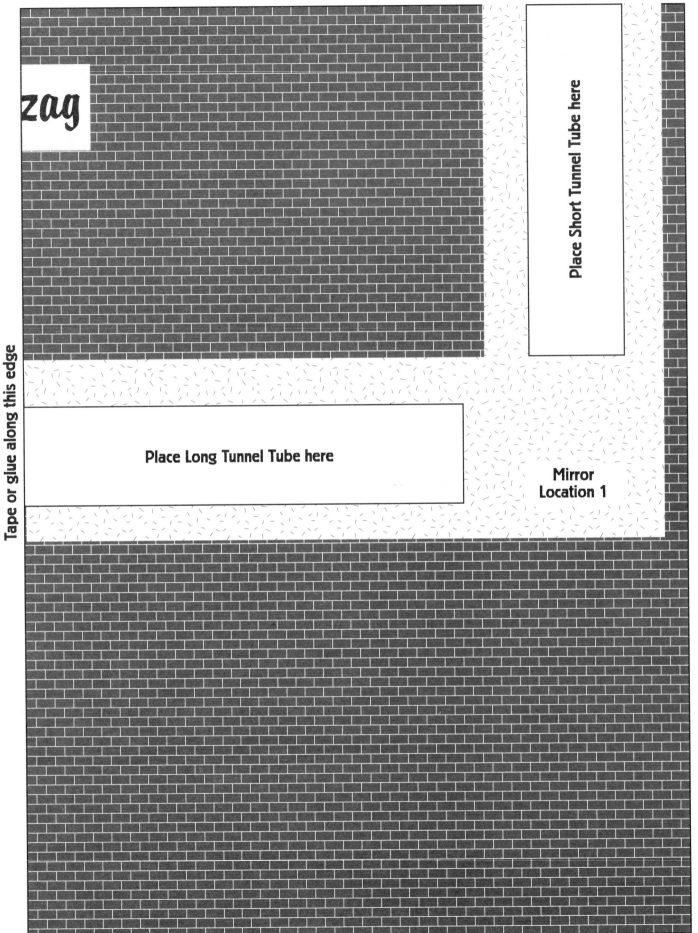

zag

Tape or glue along this edge

Place Short Tunnel Tube here

Place Long Tunnel Tube here

Mirror
Location 1

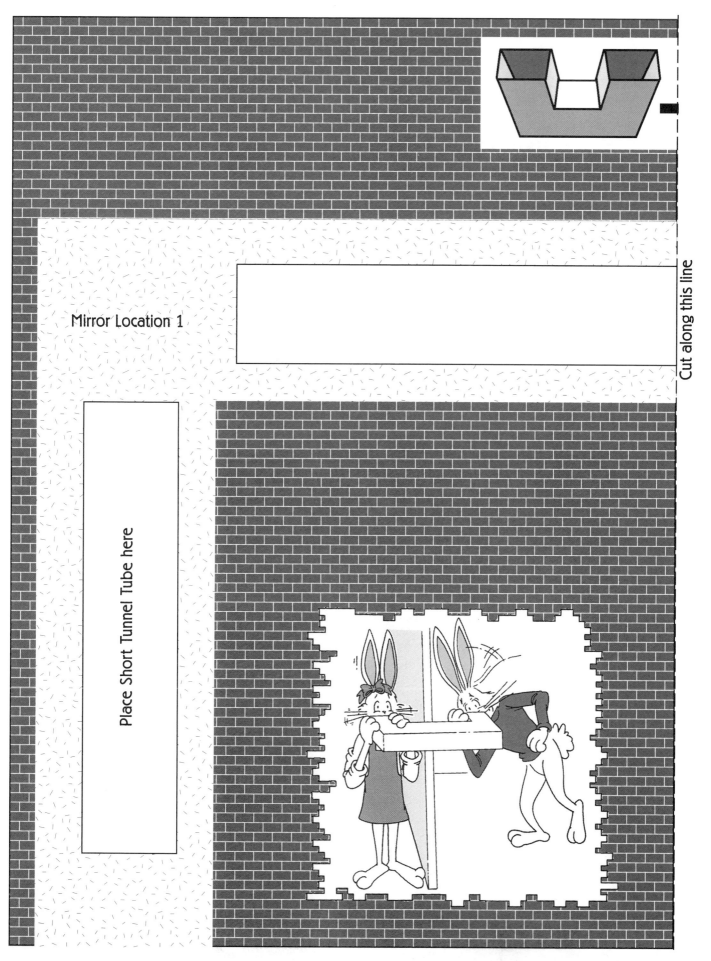

Mirror Location 1

Place Short Tunnel Tube here

Cut along this line

29

© 2000 AIMS Education Foundation

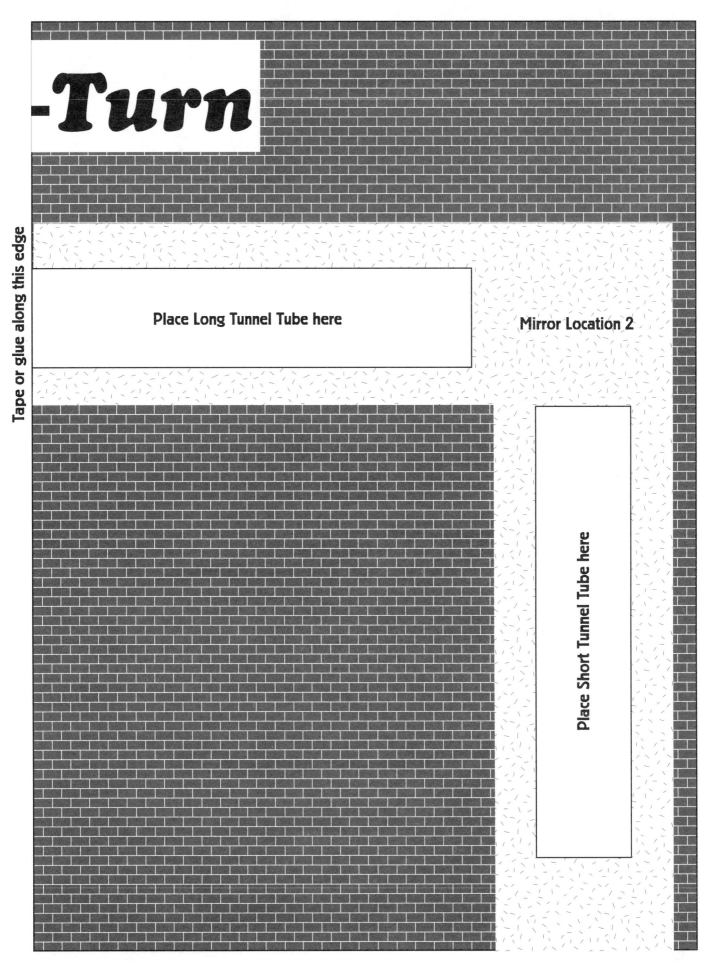

-Turn

Tape or glue along this edge

Place Long Tunnel Tube here

Mirror Location 2

Place Short Tunnel Tube here

P☉☉l Cues and Clues

Topic
Laws of plane reflection

Key Question
How are the laws that describe how light reflects off a plane mirror applied to games like pool?

Focus
Students will use a Reflect/View (a reflective, transparent plastic tool) to locate the image of a cue ball placed on a pool table. This reflected image will be used to determine the point at which the cue ball must strike the appropriate cushion so that it's reflected into a previously identified pocket.

Guiding Documents
Project 2061 Benchmark
• *...Something can be "seen" when light waves emitted or reflected by it enter the eye...*

NRC Standards
• *Light travels in a straight line until it strikes an object. Light can be reflected by a mirror, refracted by a lens, or absorbed by the object.*
• *Light interacts with matter by transmission (including refraction), absorption, or scattering (including reflection). To see an object, light from the object—emitted by or scattered from it—must enter the eye.*

NCTM Standards 2000*
• *Recognize geometric ideas and relationships and apply them to other disciplines and to problems that arise in the classroom or in everyday life*
• *Create and describe mental images of objects, patterns, and paths*
• *Select and apply appropriate standard units and tools to measure length, area, volume, weight, time, temperature, and the size of angles*

Math
Geometry and spatial sense
    constructing a perpendicular to a line
Measurement
    linear
    angle measure

Science
Physical science
    light
        plane reflection

Integrated Processes
Observing
Comparing and contrasting
Applying

Materials
For each pair of students:
    one Reflect/View or similar-sized piece of reflective, transparent plastic
    protractor
    metric ruler

Background Information
    A material object—like a ball striking a flat wall—reflects off a plane surface in the same manner that light reflects off a plane mirror. This activity will show students that the *laws of reflection* apply to many different real-world situations.
    Rabbit Ray's favorite pastime is shooting a game of pool with Raylynn. Ray likes the game of pool because the cue ball and numbered balls bounce off the sides of the pool table in the same way a light ray "bounces" off plane mirrors.
    Other games in which a ball bounces off a plane surface are tennis, table tennis, basketball, and racquet ball.
    The skills needed to play pool with Rabbit Ray are covered in the *Warm-Up Game* pages.
    This activity is an application of the two basic laws governing plane mirror reflection:
1. The line connecting the object and its mirror image is perpendicular to the mirror and the image appears to be as far behind the mirror as the object is in front of the mirror.
2. The angle of incidence equals the angle of reflection. (For simplicity, the angle of incidence and reflection are measured from the reflecting line rather than the normal.)

Management
1. It is important that you do the *Warm-Up Game* student pages before attempting this activity with students.
2. Organize students into groups of two and let them take turns using the Reflect/View.
3. Make certain that students align their Reflect/View with the interior cushion on the pool table. The proper alignment can be checked by asking students to look down directly over the Reflect/View. The interior cushion line should not be visible. (Refer to #1 in *Warm-Up Game*.)

31   © 2000 AIMS Education Foundation

Procedure

1. Distribute *Warm-Up Game* pages to every student. Instruct the students to stand the Reflect/View vertically along the line labeled *cushion 1* on the large pool table at the top of the first student page.
2. Tell the students to observe the image of the cue ball through the Reflect/View and use a pencil to mark the location of this image.
3. Have the students remove the Reflect/View and draw the straight line between the cue ball and the image of the cue ball. Have them use their protractor to measure and record the angle at A. Then ask them to measure and record the distance from the cue ball to the cushion and the distance from the image of the cue ball to the cushion. Ask them to record their comparison of these two distances on the student pages.
4. Tell the students to use their ruler to draw the line between the image of the cue ball and the black target pocket.
5. Instruct them to mark the point where this line crosses *cushion 1* and to then draw a line from the cue ball to this point. Have them draw a cue stick along this line indicating the direction of their shot.
6. Direct the students to use their protractor to measure and record the angle of incidence and the angle of reflection. Then have them compare the two angles.
7. Distribute *The Pool Problems* pages. Have students solve the two problems.
8. Distribute the *A Challenge for Experts* page.

Discussion

1. How is a pool table cushion *like* a mirror? [The cushion reflects the cue ball according to the same laws that govern how a mirror reflects light.]
2. How is a pool table cushion *different* from a mirror? [A pool table cushion is a horizontal line whereas a mirror is a plane.]
3. What other examples can you think of besides light and pool balls that deal with reflections? [radar signals (really a form of "light"), sound waves (echoes), SONAR, heat energy, water waves (Play with an eyedropper and a small container of water on the overhead.)]

Extension

Use the method to reflect the cue ball off *three* cushions.

Solution

To solve *A Challenge for Experts*, simply apply the method *twice*. The following diagrams show how. First, with the Reflect/View along *cushion 1*, find the location of the image. Mark this point with a heavy dot.

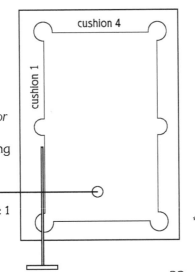

Place the Reflect/View along *cushion 4* and locate the image of *image 1*. Call this second image, *image 2*.

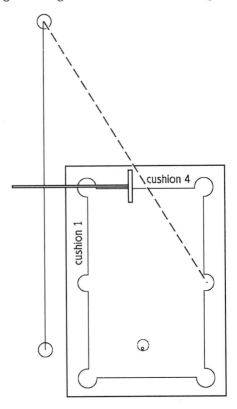

Remove the Reflect/View and draw a straight line connecting *image 2* to the black pocket. Label the point, where this line intersects *cushion 4, A*.

Draw the straight line between point *A* and *image 1*. Label the point where this line intersects *cushion 1, B*. Connect point *B* to the cue ball. Draw the cue stick along the line between the cue ball and point *B* to complete the solution.

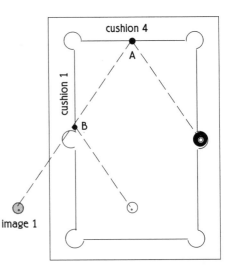

*   Reprinted with permission from *Principles and Standards for School Mathematics*, 2000 by the National Council of Teachers of Mathematics. All rights reserved.

P🎱ol Cues and Clues

Warm-Up Game

Problem: At what point on cushion 1 must the cue ball strike so that it's reflected into the black target pocket?

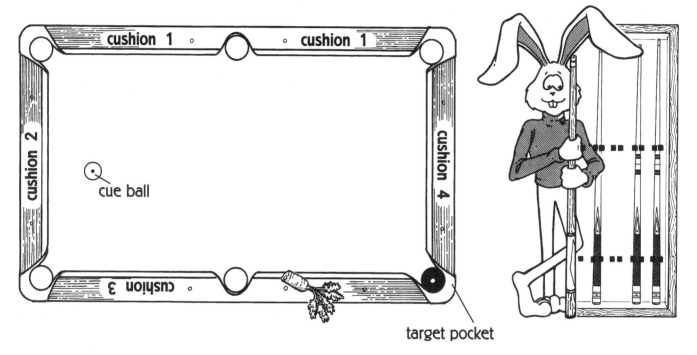

target pocket

① Stand the Reflect/View vertically along the line labeled cushion 1.

② Observe the image of the cue ball through the Reflect/View. Mark the location of the observed image.

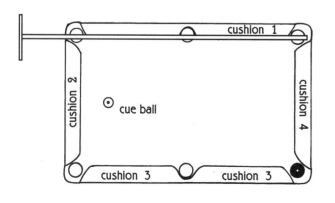

⊙ image of cue ball

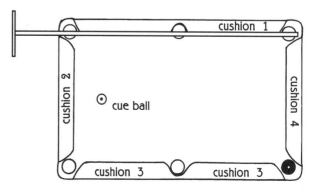

P⊚⊛l Cues and Clues
Warm-Up Game

③ Draw the line between the object and its image. This line should be perpendicular to the cushion line.
Measure the angle at A with a protractor.
∠ A = _____ °
Measure the distance from the cue ball to the cushion line. _____ cm
Measure the distance from the image of the cue ball to the cushion line. _____ cm
How do the two distances compare?

_____

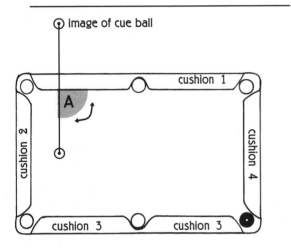

④ Draw the line from the image of the cue ball to the black target pocket.

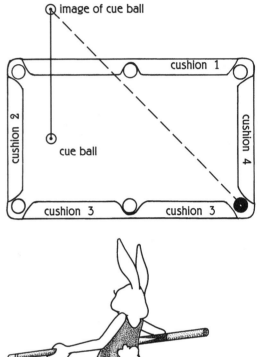

⑤ Mark the point where the line connecting the image of the cue ball with the black target pocket crosses the cushion line.
Draw a line from the cue ball to this point.
Draw the cue stick so that it is aimed along this line.

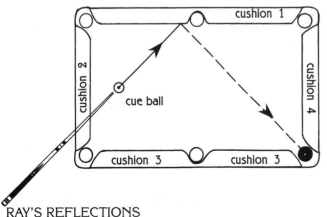

⑥ Use a protractor to measure the angle of incidence and compare its measure to the measure of the angle of reflection.
∠ I = ∠ Incidence = _____ °
∠ R = ∠ Reflection = _____ °
How do the two angles compare?

_____

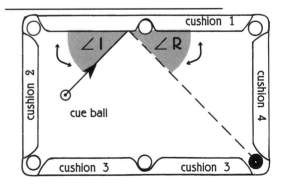

© 2000 AIMS Education Foundation

P🎱ol Cues and Clues
Pool Problems

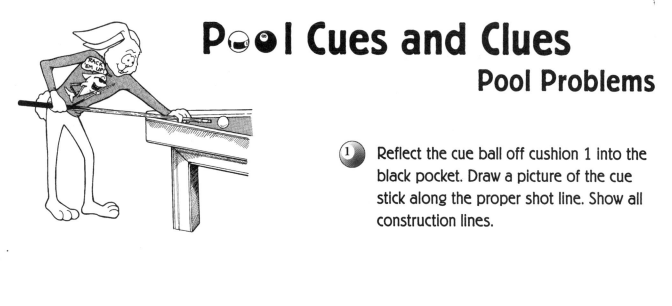

1 Reflect the cue ball off cushion 1 into the black pocket. Draw a picture of the cue stick along the proper shot line. Show all construction lines.

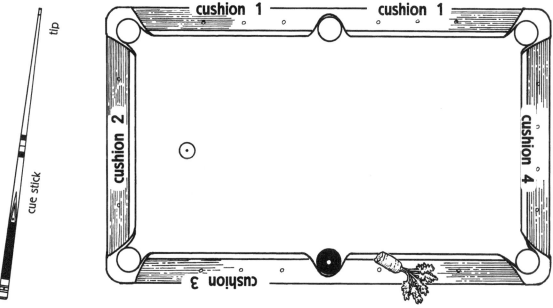

Draw the line between the object and its image. This line should be perpendicular to the cushion line. Label the point where these lines intersect A. Measure the angle at A with a protractor.

∠ A = _____ °

Measure the distance from the cue ball to the cushion line. _____ cm

Measure the distance from the image of the cue ball to the cushion line. _____ cm

How do the two distances compare?

Use a protractor to measure the angle of incidence and compare its measure to the measure of the angle of reflection.

∠ I = ∠ Incidence = _____ °

∠ R = ∠ Reflection = _____ °

How do the two angles compare?

P⊖●l Cues and Clues

Pool Problems

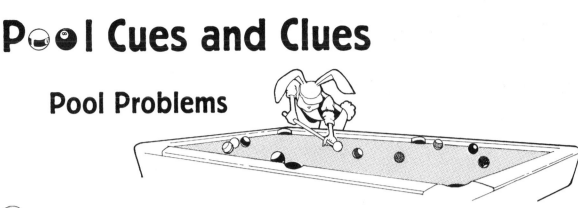

(2) Reflect the cue ball off cushion 4 into the black pocket. Draw a picture of the cue stick along the proper shot line. Show all construction lines.

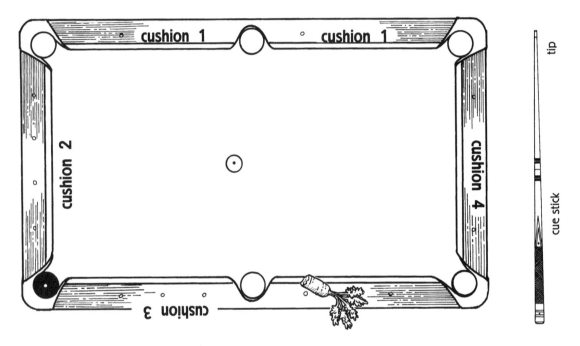

Draw the line between the object and its image. This line should be perpendicular to the cushion line. Label the point where these lines intersect A. Measure the angle at A with a protractor.

$$\angle A = \underline{\hspace{1cm}}°$$

Measure the distance from the cue ball to the cushion line. _____ cm

Measure the distance from the image of the cue ball to the cushion line. _____ cm

How do the two distances compare?

Use a protractor to measure the angle of incidence and compare its measure to the measure of the angle of reflection.

$$\angle I = \angle \text{ Incidence } = \underline{\hspace{1.5cm}}°$$

$$\angle R = \angle \text{ Reflection } = \underline{\hspace{1.5cm}}°$$

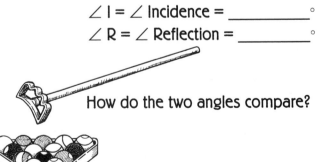

How do the two angles compare?

P⊗⊙l Cues and Clues
A Challenge for Experts

Reflect the cue ball off cushion 1, then cushion 4 into the black pocket.
Draw a picture of the cue stick along the proper shot line. Show all
construction lines.

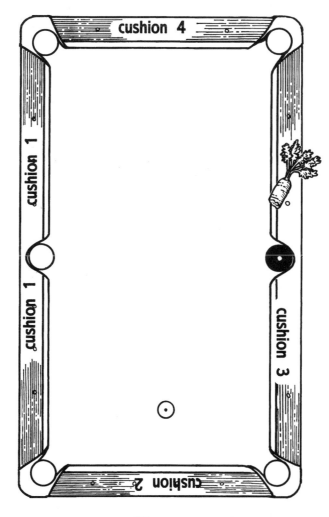

NOSE TO NOSE

The reflection that you see in a mirror is called a virtual image. This virtual image appears to be the same distance behind the mirror as the distance you are in front of the mirror. The light from your face travels to the mirror and then back to your eye. Your brain interprets this as meaning the virtual image is twice the distance of the mirror away.

The front surface of a Reflect/View acts as a mirror. Because the Reflect/View is transparent, you can also see through it, allowing you to see actual objects which are behind it. Your brain simply superimposes the real object and the virtual image. The result is that you can see your finger touch the ghostly image of your reflection. In fact, if you like, you can stick your hand inside the ghostly head with no damage.

Imagineers have used this visual trick to amuse guests in theme parks. As you ride through a haunted house, ghosts appear to be dancing in a large hall. The ghostly images are actually dancing on a transparent sheet of glass much like the Reflect/View. Through the glass, a large hall can be seen. The brain superimposes the ghosts and the hall, making the brightly lit dancing robots under the ride's track seem to be waltzing around the space in the hall.

Maybe you can create an amusing view through the Reflect/View that combines the real object behind the Reflect/View and the virtual image being reflected.

Materials
Mirror
Reflect/View

Procedure
1. Hold a mirror in front of your face.
2. Without touching your own nose, try to scratch the nose of your reflection.
3. If you cannot do it, move the mirror closer (or farther away) until you can.
4. Use a Reflect/View to try to scratch the nose of your reflected image.

Discussion
1. Could you scratch your reflection's nose without scratching your actual nose?
2. Where does your reflection appear to be in relation to the mirror?
3. When you touched the nose of your reflected image, where was the Reflect/View in relationship to your face?…your finger?
4. Why can you scratch your nose when using the Reflect/View, but not when using the mirror?

　　　　　　　　38　　　　　© 2000 AIMS Education Foundation

PUT YOUR FINGER ON RAY

Topic
Plane mirror reflection

Key Question
Where does the image in a mirror appear to be located?

Focus
Students will locate the mirror image of an object by placing a pencil on the image as seen in the mirror.

Guiding Documents
Project 2061 Benchmark
* *...Something can be "seen" when light waves emitted or reflected by it enter the eye...*

NRC Standard
* *Light interacts with matter by transmission (including refraction), absorption, or scattering (including reflection). To see an object, light from the object— emitted by or scattered from it— must enter the eye.*

NCTM Standards 2000*
* *Recognize geometric ideas and relationships and apply them to other disciplines and to problems that arise in the classroom or in everyday life*
* *Select and apply appropriate standard units and tools to measure length, area, volume, weight, time, temperature, and the size of angles*

Math
Geometry and spatial sense
    line segment
    perpendicular
Estimating

Science
Physical science
    light
        plane reflection

Integrated Processes
Observing
Comparing and contrasting

Materials
For each group:
    plane mirror
    clay, wood block, or binder clip
    one *Rabbit Ray Stand-up Figure*
    pencil
    centimeter ruler
    Angle Fixer—Right Angle

Background Information
This activity is designed to focus the student's attention on the fact that the *image* of an object, as seen in a plane mirror, **appears to be behind the mirror!** Typically, learners haven't thought about this fact. This activity should raise the question, where is the image located? Obviously, if the student looks behind the mirror for the image, it won't be found.

What's going on? Light rays are reflected off an object in all directions. Look at just one of these rays, position *A*, in the diagram.

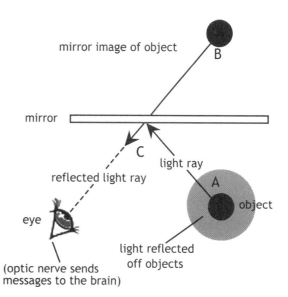

This ray strikes the mirror at point *C* and is reflected to the eye. The eye *senses* the reflected ray, "sees" that it's coming from the direction of the *mirror image* and transmits this information to the brain. The brain, being told that the light ray is coming from a known direction, "sees" the light ray as coming from that direction!

The light travels the straight line path *A* to *C* which is reflected in the mirror as the path *B* to *C*, which is equivalent in length. The image therefore *appears* as if it is located behind the mirror.

Experiencing and thinking about this phenomenon is necessary before answering the questions related to the relationships between the object and the position of the reflected image. The students are given the opportunity to think about these relationships when they use a centimeter ruler to measure and compare object and image distances from the mirror using the lines they've drawn, and use a right-angled *Angle Fixer* to *compare* the angles at which the lines cross the mirror line.

Later, more precise activities will establish the law of plane reflection that states that the straight line connecting an object with its mirror image is perpendicular to the mirror and the distance from the object to the mirror equals the distance of the image from the mirror.

Management

1. Group the students in pairs.
2. Make the *Rabbit Ray Stand-up Figures* before the activity or have students make their own figures. Show students how to grip and accurately position the figures. Be sure they know to match the short vertical line at the bottom center of the figure to the short vertical line printed on the page. If necessary, give students time to practice this.
3. Cut out the *Angle Fixers* before doing the activity or have students cut and trim them. Use the instructions at the top of the *Angle Fixer* page to explain to students how to use the *Angle Fixers*. Be sure they understand that they will use them to make comparisons, not measurements. Phrases like "they're about the same" are appropriate for describing a comparison.

Procedure

1. Distribute the materials. It's helpful to have the students tape the student pages to their table or desk tops. Assist the students in setting up their mirrors in a vertical position.
2. Instruct one student in each group to place a stand-up figure at the point labeled *A* on the student page.
3. Have the students place their eyes close to the paper, look toward the mirror, and observe the *image* of the stand-up figure in the mirror.
4. Instruct them to raise their heads until the top of the *mirror image* of the stand-up figure just touches the top of the mirror.
5. Tell them to hold their pencils straight up and down and place the tip of their pencils "on the top" of the *mirror image*.
6. Now, instruct them to lower their pencils straight down and mark the spots their pencils touch the paper by twirling the pencils between their fingers. Have the students label their points *a*.

7. Have the students take turns repeating this procedure for stand-up figure positions *B* and *C*.
8. Tell the students to use their rulers to draw the lines connecting point *A* to point *a*, point *B* to point *b*, and point *C* to point *c*.
9. Have the students label the point where each line crosses the mirror line *x*.
10. Have the students compare the distances.
11. Have the students compare the angle at which the lines connecting each stand-up figure to its image cross the mirror line. They do this by placing the right-angled corner of their *Angle Fixer* in each crossing angle and *comparing* the crossing angle to the right-angled *Angle Fixer*.

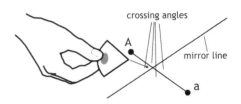

Discussion

1. Did you find a relationship between the distance an object is positioned in front of a mirror and the distance the *image* of the object appears to be located behind the mirror? Explain.
2. Did you find a relationship between the angles which the lines connecting the object and image cross the mirror? Explain.
3. Hang a large mirror on a wall near a doorway. Ask a student to stand in front of the mirror and to look at his or her image in the mirror. Ask the student these questions:
   a. Where are you? [in front of the wall]
   b. Where is the mirror? [on the wall]
   c. Where does your image *appear* to be located? [on the other side of the wall]
   d. Where, actually, is your image? [at the surface of the mirror]

Extensions

1. Substitute a Reflect/View for the mirror and have students repeat the activity.
2. Ask the students to describe how a mirror and a Reflect/View are alike and how they are different.

*   Reprinted with permission from *Principles and Standards for School Mathematics*, 2000 by the National Council of Teachers of Mathematics. All rights reserved.

Rabbit Ray Stand-up Figures

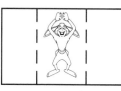

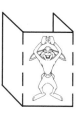

Instructions

1. Cut out the figure of Rabbit Ray along the solid lines.

2. Fold the sides of the figure along the dashed lines.

3. The figure can be easily positioned by grasping it along the folded edge.

4. This symbol represents the top view of a Stand-up Rabbit Ray figure.

Copy onto card stock.

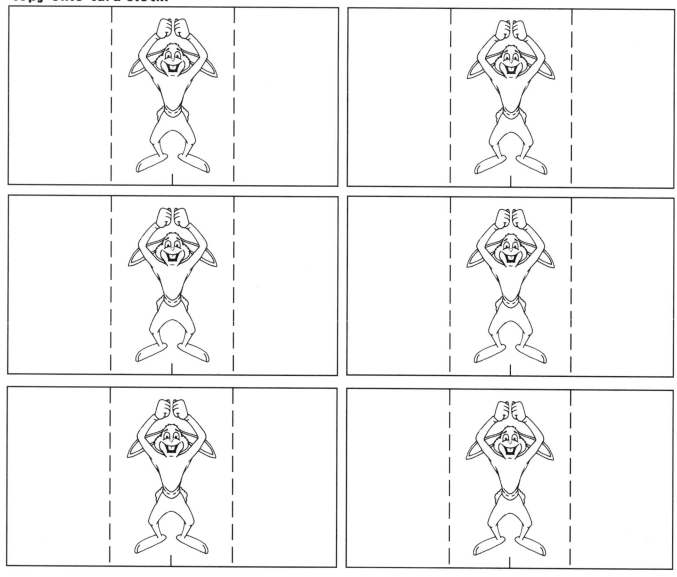

© 2000 AIMS Education Foundation

PUT YOUR FINGER ON RAY

1. Compare the line segments:

$\overline{AX}$ = _____ mm	$\overline{aX}$ = _____ mm

$\overline{BX}$ = _____ mm	$\overline{bX}$ = _____ mm

$\overline{CX}$ = _____ mm	$\overline{cX}$ = _____ mm

2. Use your Angle Fixer to compare the angles at which the lines connecting each pair of points cross the mirror.

How do they compare?

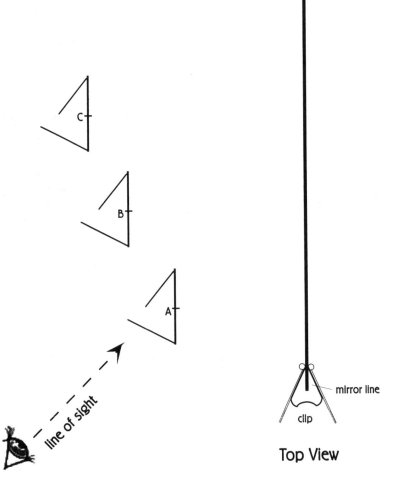

line of sight

mirror line

clip

Top View

© 2000 AIMS Education Foundation

Angle Fixer— Right Angles

Each Angle Fixer, when compared to the shaded angle it's shown on, is:

Fit the Angle Fixer in the angle to be compared.

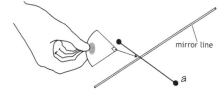

mirror line

a

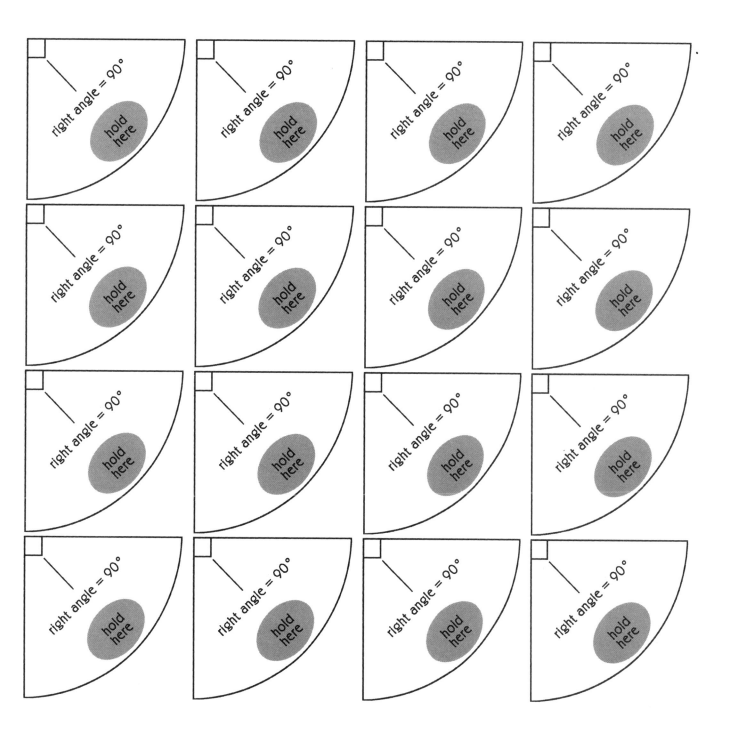

1. Less than the angle   2. Greater than the angle   3. Equal to the angle

Topic
Reflection, mirror images

Key Question
Where is an object's reflected image?

Focus
Students will use a plane mirror to investigate how far beyond the mirror the mirror image of an object lies.

Guiding Documents
Project 2061 Benchmark
- *...Something can be "seen" when light waves emitted or reflected by it enter the eye...*

NRC Standards
- *Light travels in a straight line until it strikes an object. Light can be reflected by a mirror, refracted by a lens, or absorbed by the object.*
- *Light interacts with matter by transmission (including refraction), absorption, or scattering (including reflection). To see an object, light from the object—emitted by or scattered from it—must enter the eye.*

NCTM Standards 2000*
- *Recognize geometric ideas and relationships and apply them to other disciplines and to problems that arise in the classroom or in everyday life*
- *Select and apply appropriate standard units and tools to measure length, area, volume, weight, time, temperature, and the size of angles*

Math
Measurement
    length
Geometry and spatial sense
    symmetry

Science
Physical science
    light
        plane reflection

Integrated Processes
Observing
Collecting and recording data
Comparing and contrasting
Generalizing

Materials
For each group:
    small mirror with binder clip support
    metric ruler
    2 *Rabbit Ray Stand-up Figures*

Background Information
The straight line connecting the position of an object placed in front of a plane mirror and the position of its mirror image is always perpendicular (forms a 90°, right angle) with the line marking the position of the reflecting surface. Furthermore, the distance the mirror image appears to be located behind the mirror is always equal to the distance the object is positioned in front of the mirror.

In the diagram, the line segment AB is perpendicular to the line that locates the reflecting surface. The line segment AC equals the line segment BC.

Top View

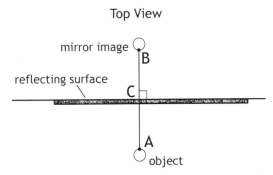

In this activity, the perpendicular line is established by using the side edge of the mirror. This makes it easy to move an object placed behind the mirror along this perpendicular until it combines with the mirror image as seen from the front of the mirror. The distances can then be measured and compared.

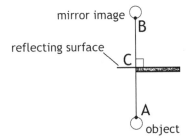

Management
1. This investigation can be done in small groups.
2. Copy the *Rabbit Ray Stand-up Figures* onto card stock.
3. Be sure students follow directions precisely, but remember, looking for reasons why results vary can be an excellent learning experience in itself.

4. Have students record observations in pencil, so that they can remeasure and correct inaccuracies if they occur.

Procedure

1. Instruct the students to place a mirror on edge on the center line of the activity sheet with the reflecting surface on the line. (Show them, if necessary, how to support the mirror by attaching a binder clip so that it stands perpendicular to the paper.) Inform the students that the left end of the mirror should just touch the broken line. Urge all students to perform the following check before proceeding:
   If the mirror image of the line at the bottom of the page lines up with the line at the top of the page, the mirror is perpendicular to the paper.

2. For *Test A*, tell students to place a Rabbit Ray figure at point A. Explain that with one eye closed, they should move their heads so that they see only the right half of the figure in the mirror.

3. Direct the students to position a second Rabbit Ray figure on the broken line behind the mirror so that it forms a full Rabbit Ray together with the image.

4. Have them measure the distance from the center (reflecting surface) line to the front of the stand-up figure. Encourage them to make measurements accurate to the nearest millimeter.

5. Direct the students to enter the information in the table and compare the distances.

6. For *Test B*, have students place a stand-up figure at point B, and repeat steps 2-5.

7. For *Test C*, have them place a stand-up figure at a location of their choice that is beyond the bottom edge of their paper but in line with the extension of the broken line, and repeat steps 2-5.

Discussion

1. Do all groups have the same measurements for each test? Why or why not?
2. Were the results of this investigation what you thought they would be? Explain.
3. Did anyone have to remeasure? Why?
4. How can we do *Test C* accurately? Is there any limit on how far from the mirror we place the Rabbit Ray figure? Explain.
5. Where is the figure's image? How do you know?
6. Would it matter if we used the right side of the mirror instead of the left? Explain.
7. What do you think would happen if the mirror were curved instead of flat?

Extensions

1. Have students color one Rabbit Ray figure by filling in the left side of his sweater and another Rabbit Ray figure by filling in the right side of his sweater. Ask students to predict what they will see in the mirror. (Will Ray's sweater, as seen in the mirror, be completely colored in?)

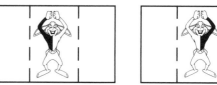

2. Have students use a Reflect/View to check their work.
3. Read to the class all or part of *Alice in Wonderland* by Lewis Carroll or another book involving mirrors.

---

* Reprinted with permission from *Principles and Standards for School Mathematics,* 2000 by the National Council of Teachers of Mathematics. All rights reserved.

Rabbit Ray Stand-up Figures

Instructions

1. Cut out the figure of Rabbit Ray along the solid lines.

2. Fold the sides of the figure along the dashed lines.

3. The figure can be easily positioned by grasping it along the folded edge.

4. This symbol represents the top view of a Stand-up Rabbit Ray figure.

Copy onto card stock.

Where is Ray's Image Located?

Place a mirror on edge on the center line of the investigation sheet with the reflecting surface on the line. Support the mirror by attaching a binder clip as illustrated so that it stands perpendicular to the paper. The left end of the mirror should just touch the broken line.

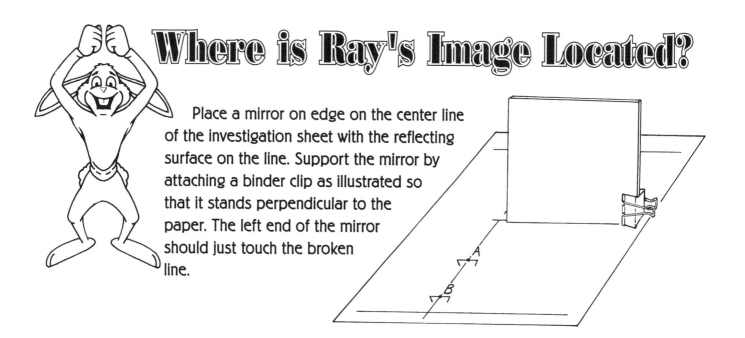

If the mirror image of the line at the bottom of the page lines up with the line at the top of the page, the mirror is perpendicular to the paper. Complete this check before proceeding.

Test A:
1. Place a Rabbit Ray figure at point A. Close one eye and move your head so that you see only the right half of the figure in the mirror.
2. Position a second Rabbit Ray figure on the broken line behind the mirror, so that it will form a complete Rabbit Ray figure together with the image.
3. Measure the distance from the center (mirror) line to the front of the Rabbit Ray figure. Make the measurements to the nearest millimeter.
4. Enter the information in the table and compare the distances.

Test B:
1. Place a Rabbit Ray figure at point B and repeat the steps of Test A, steps 2 through 4.

Test C:
1. Place a Rabbit Ray figure at a location of your choice that is beyond the bottom edge of your paper but in line with the extension of the broken line. Repeat the process.

Where's Rabbit Ray's Image?

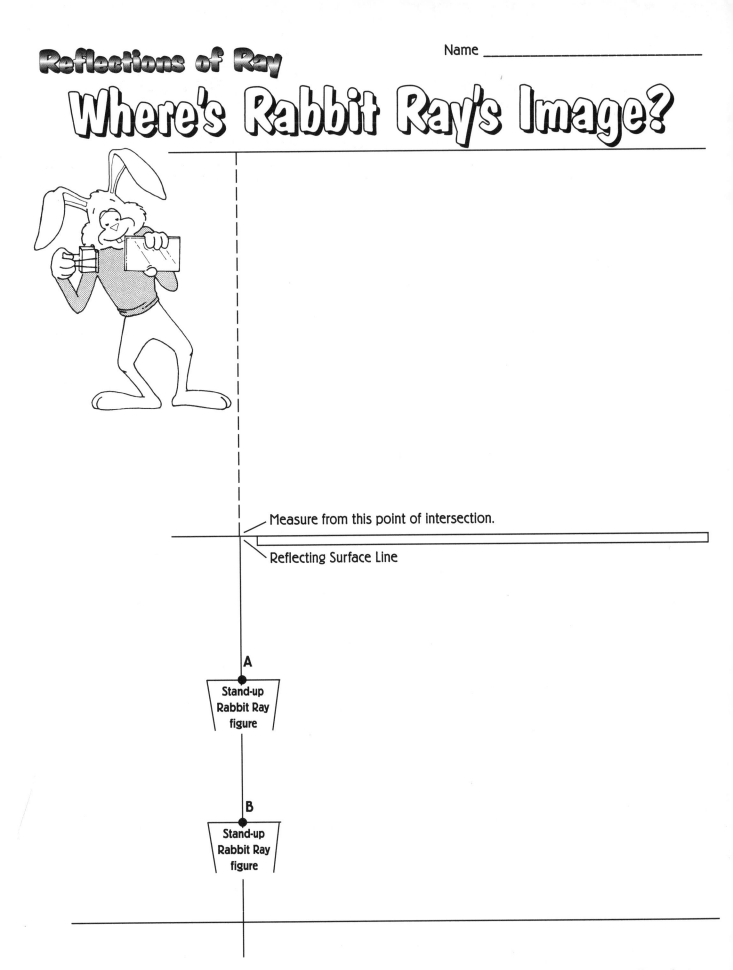

Measure from this point of intersection.

Reflecting Surface Line

A
Stand-up
Rabbit Ray
figure

B
Stand-up
Rabbit Ray
figure

48   © 2000 AIMS Education Foundation

Reflections of Ray Results

Measurement Results

Test	Distance from the front of the figure to the reflecting surface	Distance from the figure's image to the reflecting surface	Difference
A			
B			
C			

1. How do the distances in each test compare?

2. What conclusion can you draw from this investigation?

3. Why must the mirror be perpendicular to the paper?

4. Record your team's observations and discuss the results.

49 © 2000 AIMS Education Foundation

Line of Sight

Topic
Plane mirror reflection

Key Question
Where does the mirror image of an object placed in front of a plane mirror appear to be located?

Focus
Students will place an object in front of a plane mirror. They will then align two different rows of figures (one row on the left side of the object and the other row on the right side of the object) with the mirror image of the object. The intersection of the lines, when extended beyond the mirror, locates the apparent position of the mirror image.

Guiding Documents
Project 2061 Benchmark
- *...Something can be "seen" when light waves emitted or reflected it enter the eye...*

NRC Standards
- *Light travels in a straight line until it strikes an object. Light can be reflected by a mirror, refracted by a lens, or absorbed by the object.*
- *Light interacts with matter by transmission (including refraction), absorption, or scattering (including reflection). To see an object, light from that object—emitted or scattered from it—must enter the eye.*

NCTM Standards 2000*
- *Recognize geometric ideas and relationships and apply them to other disciplines and to problems that arise in the classroom or in everyday life*
- *Use geometric models to solve problems in other areas of mathematics, such as number and measurement*
- *Select and apply appropriate standard units and tools to measure length, area, volume, weight, time, temperature, and the size of angles*

Math
Geometry
    intersecting lines
Spatial sense

Science
Physical science
    light
        plane reflection

Integrated Processes
Observing
Collecting and recording data
Comparing and contrasting
Generalizing

Materials
For each group:
    plane mirror
    binder clip for mirror support
    5 *Rabbit Ray Stand-up Figures*
    colored pencils or crayons

Background Information
    This activity uses a modified version of the triangulation technique used by land surveyors, fire station lookouts, etc. to locate the position of an object when two different bearings, sight lines, on the object can be taken.

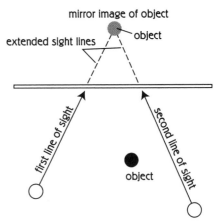

    This is a very general method for locating the position of the mirror image of an object since the sight lines can be taken from any positions.

Management
1. Group the students in pairs.
2. Make the *Rabbit Ray Stand-up Figures* before the activity or have students make their own figures.

Procedure
1. Give students time to color the shirts of each *Rabbit Ray Stand-up Figure*. They will need one each of yellow, orange, green, blue, and purple.
2. Distribute the student page and instruct the students to tape the corners of the page to the top of the desk or table.
3. Tell the students to place the mirror on the location labeled *Mirror* on the student page.

4. Ask the students to place the yellow Rabbit Ray figure at the location labeled *Yellow Rabbit Ray*. Tell them to be sure the short vertical line at the bottom of the figure matches the short line on the symbol for the figure on the student page. Some students may find it easier to use the mirror image of the figure to align the short marks.

5. Instruct students to place the orange stand-up figure at the indicated position and carefully align its marks. Have them align the green figure with its marks.

6. Ask the students to repeat this procedure for the purple and blue stand-up figures along the second line of sight.

7. Instruct the students to record on their student pages at what the stand-up figures along the *first line of sight* are pointing. Have them do the same for the figures along the *second line of sight*.

8. Ask the students to remove their mirrors and use their rulers to extend the first and second lines of sight beyond the mirror line until they intersect at a point. Tell them to label this part B.

9. Tell them to record on their student pages what is located at the point of intersection.

10. Instruct the sutdents to draw the straight line between point A and point B.

Discussion

1. What does it mean to "point at an object"? (Find out if students understand that the common assumption made when someone points at an object is that an imaginary straight line is to be inferred to exist between the pointer and the object.)

2. At what are the green and orange figures "pointing"? [the image of the yellow figure]

3. At what are the blue and purple figures pointing? [the image of the yellow figure]

4. What is located at the *intersection* of these two "lines of sight"? [the image of the yellow figure]

5. At what angle does the line segment connecting point A with point B intersect the mirror? [90° or a right angle]

6. Compare the distance point B is behind the mirror with the distance point A is in front of the mirror.

Extension

Try sight lines, for the same object, from positions different from those printed on the student page. Do they produce different results? [no] Why? [Every sight line intersects every other sight line at the same point behind the mirror, the position of the mirror image.]

* Reprinted with permission from *Principles and Standards for School Mathematics*, 2000 by the National Council of Teachers of Mathematics. All rights reserved.

Rabbit Ray Stand-up Figures

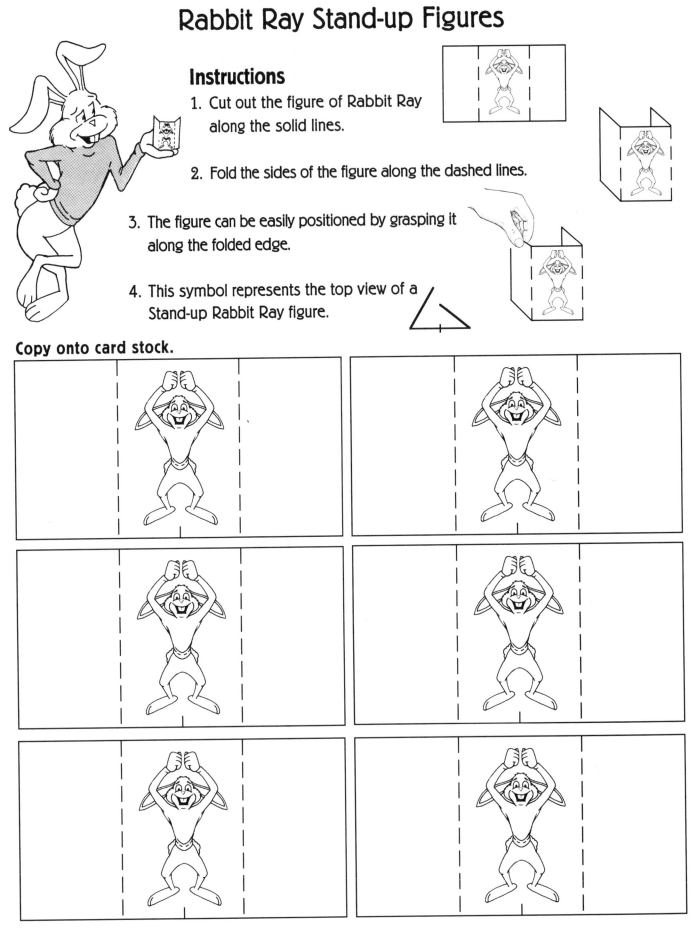

Instructions

1. Cut out the figure of Rabbit Ray along the solid lines.

2. Fold the sides of the figure along the dashed lines.

3. The figure can be easily positioned by grasping it along the folded edge.

4. This symbol represents the top view of a Stand-up Rabbit Ray figure.

Copy onto card stock.

Line of Sight

Name _____

1. At what are the green and orange figures "pointing"?

   _____

2. At what are the blue and purple figures "pointing"?

   _____

3. What is located at the intersection of the lines of sight?

   _____

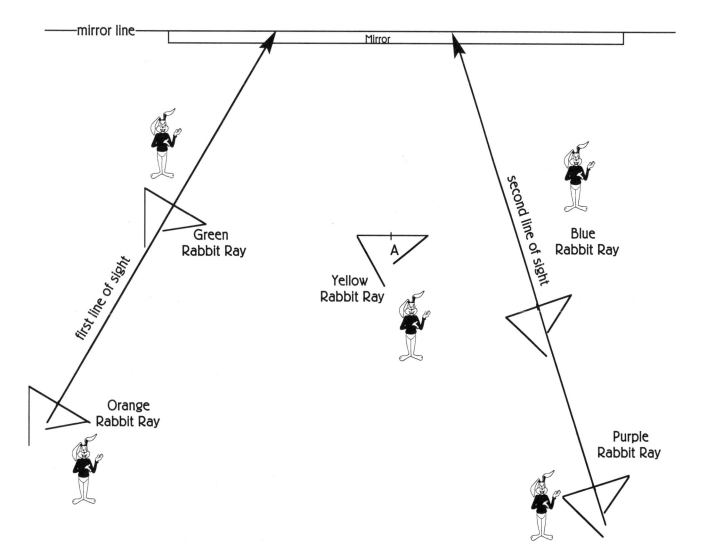

mirror line

Mirror

first line of sight

second line of sight

Green Rabbit Ray

Yellow Rabbit Ray

A

Blue Rabbit Ray

Orange Rabbit Ray

Purple Rabbit Ray

Put Your Finger on Ray, Again!

Topic
Plane mirror reflection

Key Question
How does the location of the image in a plane mirror of a fixed object change as the position of the observer changes?

Focus
The position of the mirror image is independent of the position of the observer.

Guiding Documents
Project 2061 Benchmark
- *…Something can be "seen" when light waves emitted or reflected by it enter the eye…*

NRC Standards
- *Light travels in a straight line until it strikes an object. Light can be reflected by a mirror, refracted by a lens, or absorbed by an object.*
- *Light interacts with matter by transmission (including refraction), absorption, or scattering (including reflection). To see an object, light from the object—emitted by or scattered from it—must enter the eye.*

NCTM Standard 2000*
- *Recognize geometric ideas and relationships and apply them to other disciplines and to problems that arise in the classroom or in everyday life*

Math
Geometry
    line segment
Spatial sense

Science
Physical science
    light
        plane reflection

Integrated Processes
Observing
Comparing and contrasting
Generalizing

Materials
For each group:
    binder clip for mirror support
    plane mirror
    one *Rabbit Ray Stand-up Figure*
    pencil

Background Information
The activity, *Put Your Finger On Ray*, established the fact that the mirror image of an object *appears* to be located *behind* the mirror. In that activity, the position of the observer was held constant while the position of the object was changed. This activity explores the question as to whether the position of the observer affects the position of the mirror image. Here, the position of the object—and therefore the position of the mirror image—is held constant while the position of the observer is changed.

The position of the mirror image of an object seen in a plane mirror *is determined by the distance* the object is positioned in front of the mirror as measured along a line perpendicular to the mirror.

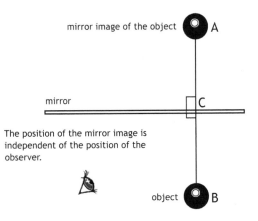

mirror image of the object ⦿ A

mirror ——————————— □ C

The position of the mirror image is independent of the position of the observer.

object ⦿ B

In the diagram, an object is located at the position labeled B. The line segment BC is perpendicular to the mirror at the position labeled C. The line segment BC is extended to the position labeled A so that $\overline{CA} = \overline{BC}$. This locates precisely the image of the object. **The only way to change the position of the image is to change the position of the object, not the observer.**

Management

1. Group the students in pairs.
2. Make the *Rabbit Ray Stand-up Figures*, use the figures from a previous activity, or have students make the figures.

Procedure

1. Distribute the materials. It's helpful to have students tape the student page to their table or desk tops. Assist the students in setting up their mirrors in a vertical position.
2. Instruct one student in each group to place a stand-up figure at the point labeled *X* on their student page.
3. Have the students place their eyes close to the paper along the line of sight labeled *A*, look toward the mirror, and observe the *image* of the stand-up figure in the mirror.
4. Instruct them to raise their heads until the top of the *mirror image* of the stand-up figure just touches the top of the mirror.
5. Tell them to hold their pencils straight up and down and place the tip of their pencils on the top of the *mirror image*.
6. Now, instruct them to lower their pencils straight down and mark the spots their pencils touch the paper by twirling the pencils between their fingers. Have the students label their points *a*.
7. Have the students take turns repeating this procedure for the line of sights labeled *B*, *C*, and *D;* labeling each point with a corresponding lower case letter.

Discussion

1. How do the positions of the pencil marks *a*, *b*, c, and *d* compare? [They are grouped close together.]
2. What does the position of the points indicate? [The position of the mirror image doesn't change (within observational error) with a change in position of the observer.]

Extensions

1. Substitute a Reflect/View for the mirror and have students repeat the activity. Ask the students which was easier to use, the mirror or the Reflect/View.
2. Put a mirror on the wall of the classroom. Ask the students to position themselves around it. Have each student describe what can be seen in the mirror. Ask how this experience relates to the activity they just did.

---

* Reprinted with permission from *Principles and Standards for School Mathematics,* 2000 by the National Council of Teachers of Mathematics. All rights reserved.

Rabbit Ray Stand-up Figures

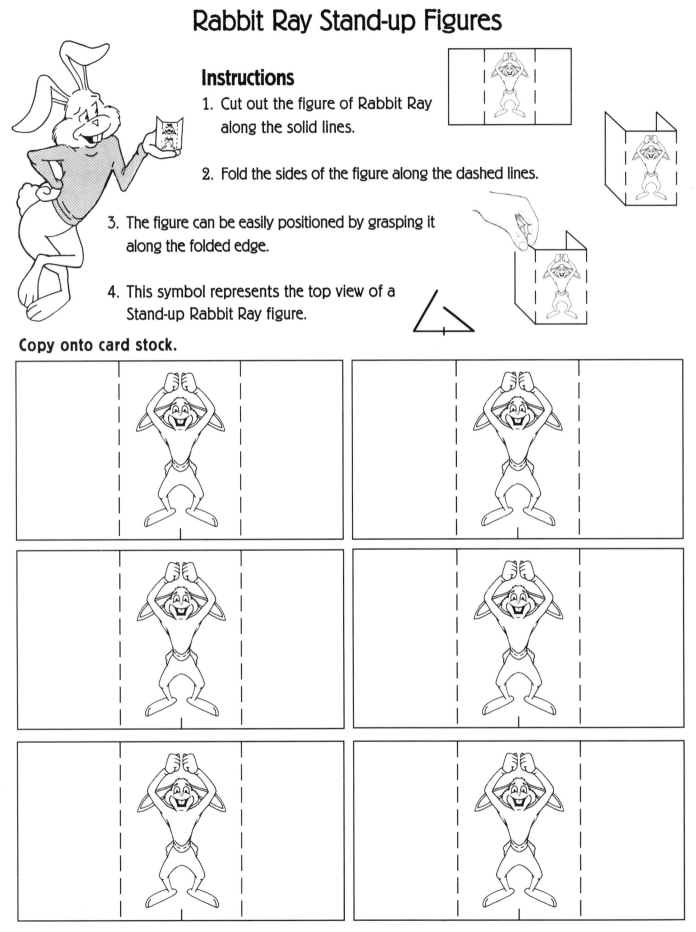

Instructions

1. Cut out the figure of Rabbit Ray along the solid lines.

2. Fold the sides of the figure along the dashed lines.

3. The figure can be easily positioned by grasping it along the folded edge.

4. This symbol represents the top view of a Stand-up Rabbit Ray figure.

Copy onto card stock.

Put Your Finger on Ray, Again!

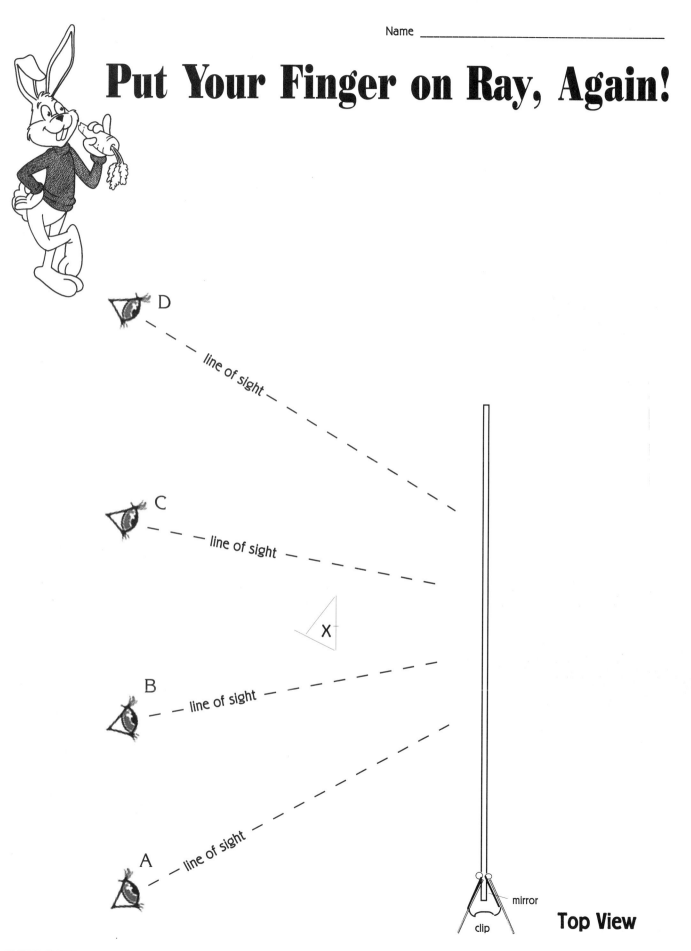

D

line of sight

C

line of sight

X

B

line of sight

A

line of sight

mirror

clip

Top View

57   © 2000 AIMS Education Foundation

Topic
Plane mirror reflection

Key Question
Where does your mirror image appear to be located?

Focus
Students will use a small mirror to investigate how far away their images appear to be located.

Guiding Documents
Project 2061 Benchmark
- *...Something can be "seen" when light waves emitted or reflected by it enter the eye...*

NRC Standards
- *Light travels in a straight line until it strikes an object. Light can be reflected by a mirror, refracted by a lens, or absorbed by the object.*
- *Light interacts with matter by transmission (including refraction), absorption, or scattering (including reflection). To see an object, light from the object—emitted by or scattered from it—must enter the eye.*

NCTM Standards 2000*
- *Recognize geometric ideas and relationships and apply them to other disciplines and to problems that arise in the classroom or in everyday life*
- *Select and apply appropriate standard units and tools to measure length, area, volume, weight, time, temperature, and the size of angles*

Math
Measurement
    length
Whole number operations

Science
Physical science
    light
        plane reflection

Integrated Processes
Observing
Predicting
Collecting and recording data
Comparing and contrasting
Interpreting data
Generalizing

Materials
For each student:
    activity sheets

For each group:
    3" x 5" mirror
    metric measuring tape
    masking tape

Background Information
In the previous activities that locate the position of the mirror image of an object placed in front of a plane mirror, the objects used have been small, stand-up figures of Rabbit Ray or some other substitute. In this activity, students are the "objects." This activity provides a model for students to work through and remember when they see their images in the many mirrors encountered in everyday life.

If you look directly into a mirror at the reflection of your face, you see your face because the image bounces back directly; if you were asked where your image is, you would (rightly) say it is directly in front of you, the same distance behind the mirror as you are in front. When you look at some other part of your body, this basic principle is not as obvious, although it remains just as valid.

Management
1. This investigation is done with groups of four or more students: one is the Observer, one the Image Partner, one the Measurer/Recorder, and one the Mirror Engineer.
2. Be sure the students follow directions precisely, but remember, looking for reasons why results vary can be an excellent learning experience in itself.
3. Have students record observations in pencil, so that they can remeasure and correct inaccuracies if they occur.
4. It is important for the Mirror Holder to hold the mirror flat against the side of the desk, so that it is perpendicular to the floor. If possible, tape the mirror to the desk.
5. See *Reflections of Ray* for the table-top version of this activity.

Procedure
1. Have the Mirror Engineer measure and mark with masking tape places 200, 400, and 600 centimeters from a desk, as shown on activity sheet.

2. Direct the Mirror Engineer to hold a plane mirror against the desk, perpendicular to the floor, and be prepared to move the mirror up or down as directed by the Observer.

3. Have the Observer stand with toes at the 200 centimeter mark, and direct the Mirror Engineer to raise or lower the mirror until the Observer can see his or her toes in the mirror.

4. Encourage the students to predict where the Image Partner will need to stand in order that his/her body will be aligned with the image of the Observer's toes.

5. Have the Image Partner stand on the other side of the desk, beyond the mirror, and move backward or forward as directed by the Observer until the Image Partner's toes, as viewed by the Observer, are lined up beside the mirror image of the Observer's toes.

6. Ask the Measurer/Recorder to determine and record the distance from the mirror to the Image Partner's toes, and then subtract the smaller number from the larger to find the difference.

7. Have students predict the results at 400 cm and explain their predictions. Repeat steps 2-5 using the 400 and 600 cm marks.

8. Encourage the teams to discuss their observations and try to explain their results in writing on the activity sheets.

9. In a class discussion, invite all teams to share their results.

10. Repeat the investigation using different students.

Discussion

1. Using the results of this activity, how would you answer the question: Where does your mirror image appear to be located?

2. Where did you expect the Image Partner to stand? Were you right? Why or why not?

3. Why is it important to follow directions exactly in setting up the investigation?

4. What made it hard for the Observer to see his or her toes in the mirror? Would a larger mirror have made it easier or more difficult? Why?

5. Why did results vary slightly? Did anyone catch errors and redo part of the investigation? If so, what did you learn from this?

6. Would it matter if we used the right side of the mirror instead of the left?

7. What do you think would happen if the mirror were curved instead of flat?

Home Link

Investigations such as this one which include full directions are excellent tools for involving the home in the school's curriculum, because the student does not have to remember the details of the directions. Be sure students understand that the activity can also be done in a doorway.

* Reprinted with permission from *Principles and Standards for School Mathematics,* 2000 by the National Council of Teachers of Mathematics. All rights reserved.

Behind the Looking Glass

Where does your mirror image appear to be located?

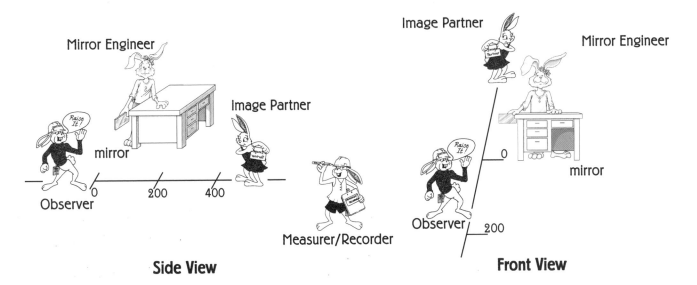

Image Partner

Mirror Engineer

Image Partner

Mirror Engineer

mirror

Raise It!

0   200   400

Observer

Measurer/Recorder

Side View

Raise It!

0

mirror

Observer   200

Front View

The Mirror Engineer measures and marks places 200, 400, and 600 centimeters from the desk (or door frame).

The Mirror Engineer holds a mirror flat against the desk (perpendicular to the floor), and is prepared to move the mirror up or down as directed by the Observer.

Raise It!

The Observer stands with toes at the 200 centimeter mark, and directs the Mirror Engineer to raise or lower the mirror until the Observer can see his or her toes in the mirror.

The Image Partner stands on the other side of the desk beyond the mirror, and moves backward or forward as directed by the observer until the Image Partner's toes, as viewed by the Observer, are lined up beside the mirror image of the Observer's toes.

The Measurer/Recorder measures and records the distance from the mirror to the Image Partner's toes. The investigation is then repeated from distances of 400 and 600 centimeters.

Behind the Looking Glass

Name _____

Team Members: 200 cm

Observer _____

Image Partner _____

Measurer/Recorder _____

Mirror Engineer _____

Measurement Results

Distance from Observer to mirror	200 cm
Distance from mirror to Image Partner	
Difference	

Discuss the results in your team and record your observations _____

_____

Team Members: 400 cm

Observer _____

Image Partner _____

Measurer/Recorder _____

Mirror Engineer _____

Measurement Results

Distance from Observer to mirror	400 cm
Distance from mirror to Image Partner	
Difference	

Discuss the results in your team and record your observations _____

_____

Team Members: 600 cm

Observer _____

Image Partner _____

Measurer/Recorder _____

Mirror Engineer _____

Measurement Results

Distance from Observer to mirror	600 cm
Distance from mirror to Image Partner	
Difference	

Discuss the results in your team and record your observations _____

_____

© 2000 AIMS Education Foundation

Looking for Ray

Topic
Plane mirror reflection

Key Questions
1. How could you determine if you can you see yourself in a mirror if you are not directly in front of a mirror?
2. How would you determine if you can you see an object other than yourself in a mirror if the object is not directly in front of the mirror?

Focus
Students will attempt to view their images in a mirror that is not directly in front of them. Students will then place objects at various locations in front of and not in front of a plane mirror. They will then determine which images of the object can be seen from a fixed position.

Guiding Documents
Project 2061 Benchmark
- *...Something can be "seen" when light waves emitted or reflected by it enter the eye...*

NRC Standards
- *Light travels in a straight line until it strikes an object. Light can be reflected by a mirror, refracted by a lens, or absorbed by an object.*
- *Light interacts with matter by transmission (including refraction), absorption, or scattering (including reflection). To see an object, light from the object—emitted by or scattered from it—must enter the eye.*

NCTM Standard 2000*
- *Recognize geometric ideas and relationships and apply them to other disciplines and to problems that arise in the classroom or in everyday life*

Math
Geometry
Spatial sense

Science
Physical science
    light
        plane reflection

Integrated Processes
Observing
Comparing and contrasting
Generalizing

Materials
For each group:
    plane mirror
    binder clip for mirror support
    one *Rabbit Ray Stand-up Figure*

Background Information
To see ourselves in a mirror, we have to be directly in front of the mirror. *Directly in front* of the mirror is defined as being anywhere within the shaded area in the diagram.

For example, every light ray reflected from my face strikes the mirror at an angle such that the rays are reflected away from my eye. In the diagram below, the lightly shaded circle represents *all* of the light rays reflected off my head. The darker shaded section represents just those rays that strike the mirror. Notice that the *angle of incidence* of every one of those rays is such that every ray will be reflected *away* from my eyes. Therefore, I cannot see my mirror image unless I am directly in front of (as defined above) the mirror.

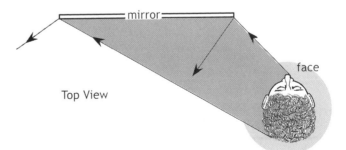

An object not directly in front of a mirror can be seen *if* the observer is properly positioned. In the next diagram, the lightly shaded circle represents the light rays reflected off an object. The diagram shows that it is now possible for light rays reflected off the object to strike the mirror at angles that will reflect them to the observers' eyes.

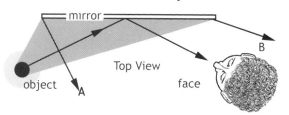

The light rays labeled *A* and *B* define the region in which the observer can see the object.

Management
1. Group the students in pairs.
2. Make the *Rabbit Ray Stand-up Figures*, use the figures from a previous activity, or have students make the figures.

Procedure
1. Distribute the materials. It's helpful to have students tape the student page to their table or desk tops. Assist them in setting up their mirrors in a vertical position.
2. Ask the students to try to see their reflections when they are not directly in front of the mirror.
3. Have them place a Rabbit Ray figure in front of the mirror at the position labeled A. Direct them to place their eyes close to the paper, along the indicated line of sight, looking toward the mirror, and observe if the *image* of the stand-up figure can be seen in the mirror.
4. Have them record their observations on their student pages.
5. Repeat steps 3 and 4 for the positions labeled B, C, and D.
6. With the Rabbit Ray figure at the position labeled D, have the students place their eyes near the position labeled E, sight along the indicated line, and record what they observe in the mirror.

Discussion
1. What did you observe in the mirror at the positions labeled A and B? [the mirror image of the figure]
2. Compare what you observed at the positions A and B with what you observed at position C. [The complete mirror images of the figure are seen at positions A and B but only half the figure can be seen in the mirror at position C.]
3. What did you observe at the position labeled D? [The figure cannot be seen.]
4. What did you observe when you looked in the mirror at the position labeled E? [I could see the image of the figure at position D.]
5. In your own words, explain in writing when you can see your image in a mirror. [When I am directly in front of the mirror.]
6. Write, again in your own words, when you can see an object other than yourself in a mirror. [I must be in a position to see those light rays reflected from the object that strike the mirror at an incident angle. In other words, I must be able to see the *reflected rays*.]

Extension
Challenge students to find the *range* of positions that they can see the image of the figure placed at position D. [The reflected rays A and B determine the positions from which the figure can be seen.]

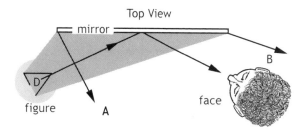

* Reprinted with permission from *Principles and Standards for School Mathematics,* 2000 by the National Council of Teachers of Mathematics. All rights reserved.

Rabbit Ray Stand-up Figures

Instructions

1. Cut out the figure of Rabbit Ray along the solid lines.

2. Fold the sides of the figure along the dashed lines.

3. The figure can be easily positioned by grasping it along the folded edge.

4. This symbol represents the top view of a Stand-up Rabbit Ray figure.

Copy onto card stock.

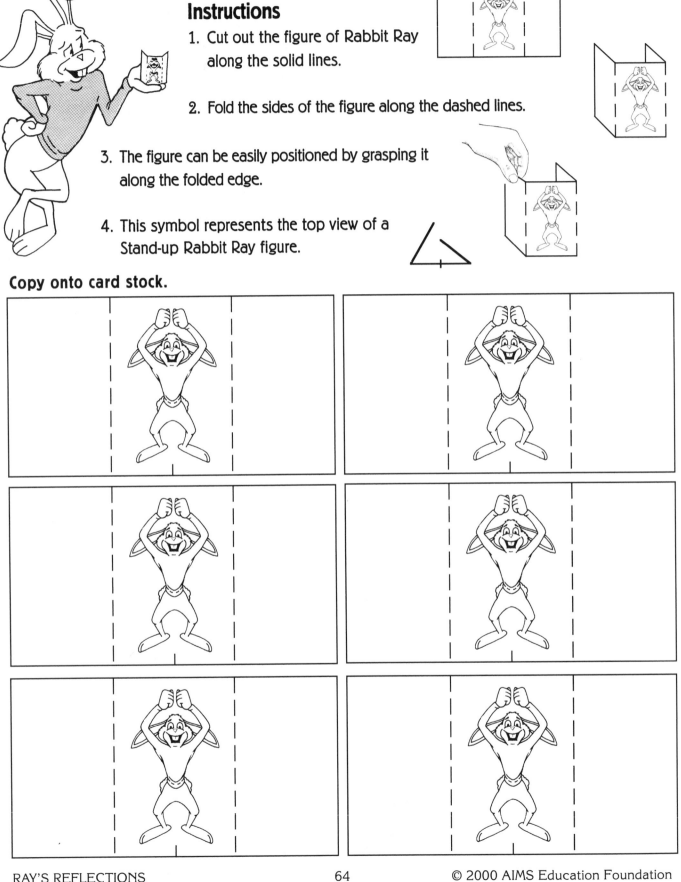

Looking for Ray

Describe how much of the mirror image can be seen from each position.

Position A _____

Position B _____

Position C _____

Position D _____

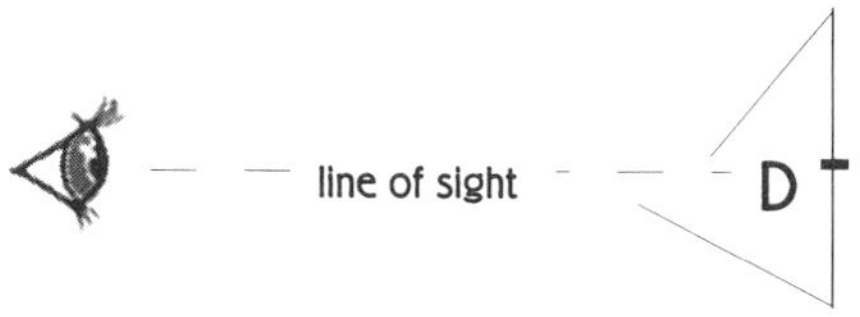

line of sight — D

Place the Rabbit Ray figure at the position labeled D. Place your eye at the position labeled E and look along the line of sight. Describe what you see.

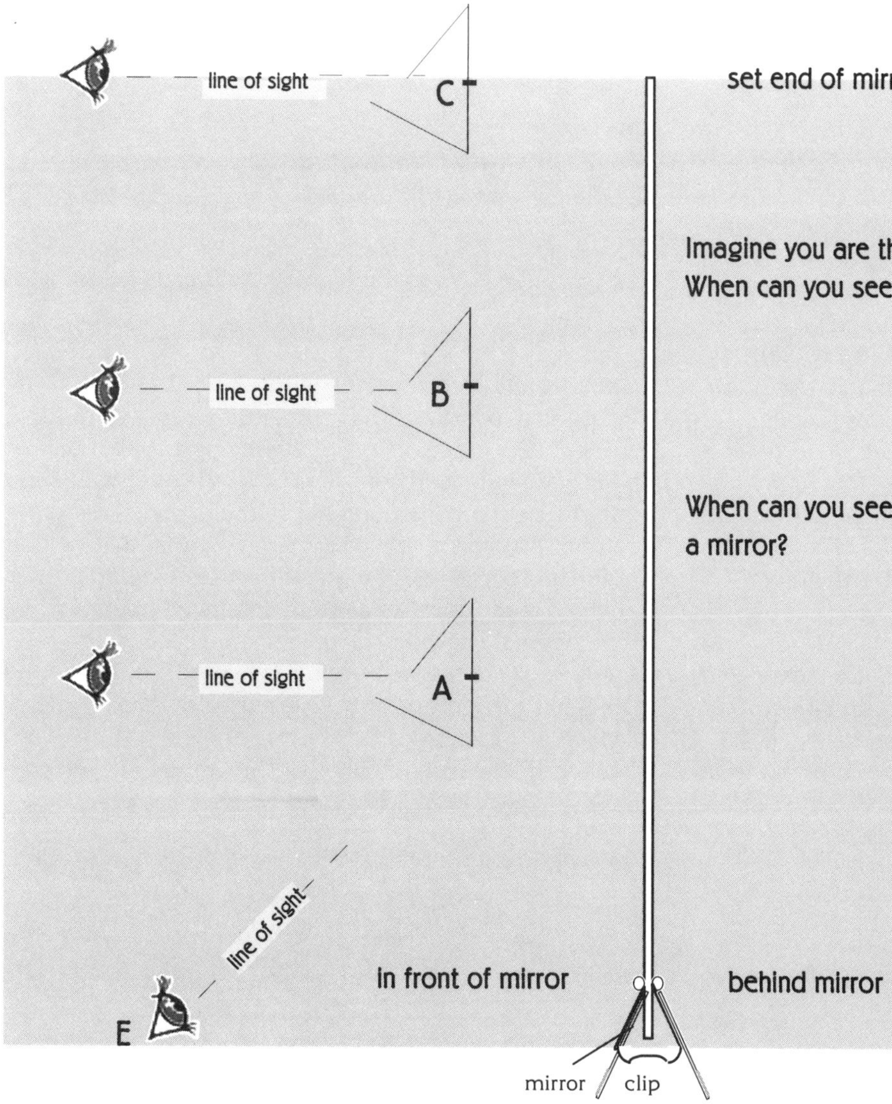

line of sight — C

set end of mirror at this position

Imagine you are the Rabbit Ray figure. When can you see your image in a mirror?

line of sight — B

When can you see the image of another object in a mirror?

line of sight — A

line of sight

in front of mirror   behind mirror

E

mirror clip

65 © 2000 AIMS Education Foundation

LIKELY

Topic
The law of plane reflection

Key Question
How is the direction at which a narrow beam of light strikes a plane mirror related to the direction the beam is reflected off it?

Focus
Students will use the narrow beam produced by a flashlight to explore how the angle at which the beam is directed towards a plane mirror is related to the angle at which the beam is reflected off the mirror.

Guiding Documents
Project 2061 Benchmarks
- *Mathematics is the study of many kinds of patterns, including numbers and shapes and operations on them. Sometimes patterns are studied because they help to explain how the world works or how to solve practical problems, sometimes because they are interesting in themselves.*
- *Numbers and shapes—and operations on them— help to describe and predict things about the world around us.*
- *Measuring instruments can be used to gather accurate information for making scientific comparisons of objects and events and for designing and constructing things that will work properly.*

NRC Standard
- *Light travels in a straight line until it strikes an object. Light can be reflected by a mirror, refracted by a lens, or absorbed by the object.*

NCTM Standards 2000*
- *Recognize geometric ideas and relationships and apply them to other disciplines and to problems that arise in the classroom or in everyday life*
- *Understand such attributes as length, area, weight, volume, and size of angle and select the appropriate type of unit for measuring each attribute*

Math
Geometry and spatial sense
   ray
   angle
Measurement
   angle
Estimating

Science
Physical science
   light
     plane reflection

Integrated Processes
Observing
Comparing and contrasting
Predicting
Generalizing

Materials
For each group of three students:
   flashlight (see *Management*)
   mirror
   binder clip for mirror support
   scissors
   ruler

Background Information
   Almost everyone has an intuitive understanding of the *law of plane reflection*. Bouncing a rubber ball off a flat wall, reflecting a basketball off the backboard and into the net, and shooting balls off cushions in a game of pool are just a few of the everyday activities that make use of the law of plane reflection. Playing games such as these soon leads to an intuitive understanding that the angle at which an object strikes a flat surface— the *angle of incidence*—equals the angle at which the object is reflected from the surface—the *angle of reflection*. In science books these angles are measured from a line perpendicular to the reflecting surface. This line is called the *normal*.

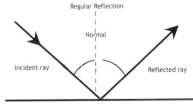

   The *normal* is useful for extending the law of reflection to surfaces that are curved. In this activity the angle of incidence and reflection will be measured from the mirror.

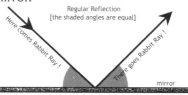

Regular Reflection
[the shaded angles are equal]

Here Comes Rabbit Ray !

There goes Rabbit Ray !

mirror

Angle measure, especially using a protractor, is difficult for students to master. In this activity students use cut-out paper angles, called *Angle Fixers*, to *compare* the incident angle to the reflected angle. *Angle Fixers* are noncustomary units of angle measure that give students the opportunity to see, touch, and move angles.

This activity helps students connect their everyday experiences with the reflection of material objects, such as balls, to the reflection of a non-material beam of light.

Management

1. Copy the *Slit Stand Patterns* page. Make one *Slit Stand* per student group. The purpose of a *Slit Stand* is to change the broad flashlight beam into a narrow beam.

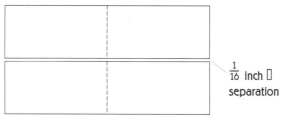

$\frac{1}{16}$ inch ☐ separation

Slit Stand Pattern

To make a Slit Stand, cut a single pattern from the page. Cut along the solid lines. Place the two strips side by side so that a 1/16 inch gap separates them. (The gap on the pattern page is 1/16 inch.)

transparent tape

Place a piece of transparent tape across the top of the two strips. Place two additional pieces of tape across the bottom half as shown in the diagram.

Fold the piece along the dashed line. Stand the piece on its base.

completed Slit Stand

2. Check the light beam of each flashlight by placing the *Slit Stand* on a piece of white paper. Turn the flashlight on and position it approximately four inches from the *Slit Stand*. Aim the light beam directly at the slit and tilt the back of the flashlight up and down to find the position that produces the best-defined beam of light.

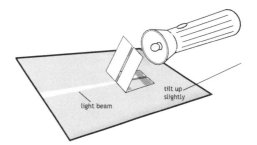

tilt up slightly

light beam

If the flashlight beam can be focused, experiment to find the focus that produces the best-defined beam. Knowing how to produce a will-defined beam will make it easier for you to help your studens.

3. Test each binder clip mirror stand to make sure that it supports the mirror as near to the vertical as possible.

4. Review for students the geometric definition of *ray* (a portion of a line starting at one point and going on in one direction) and *angle* (the figure formed by two distinct *rays* starting from the same endpoint).

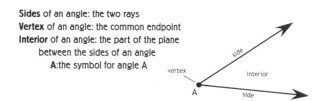

Sides of an angle: the two rays
Vertex of an angle: the common endpoint
Interior of an angle: the part of the plane between the sides of an angle
A: the symbol for angle A

vertex

side

interior

side

A

5. Describe a beam of light as a collection of light rays. Explain that the *Slit Stands* are to select only that bunch of light rays, as determined by the width of the slit, going in approximately the same direction.

Procedure

1. Instruct the students to tape the corners of their student page to the top of their desk or table.
2. Distribute one flashlight and *Slit Stand* per group.
3. Distribute a set of *Angle Fixers* for angle A, angle B, and angle C to each group and have students cut them out.
4. Turn off the room lights. Instruct the students to turn a student page over to the blank side. Tell them to place a *Slit Stand* in the center of the page. Now have them turn on the flashlights and position the flashlights about four inches from the

Slit Stand with the beam aimed at the slit. Tell them to tilt the flashlight up and down and/or move the flashlight towards or away from the *Slit Stand* until they see a well-defined beam of light on the surface of the paper.

5. Have the students stand their mirrors vertically on the blank page, about three inches behind the *Slit Stand*. Have them then aim the light beam at the *Slit Stand*, rotate the mirror from side to side, and observe the behavior of the *reflected* beam. Allow each member of the group the opportunity to "play" with the beam of light.

6. Have one student in each group place the *Slit Stand* at the position labeled A on their student pages. Tell them to direct the light beam at the *Slit Stand* along the line going from the illustrated flashlight. They should center the line in the beam of light.

7. Instruct them to now look at the reflected beam of light and to mark the middle of the *reflected* beam with a pencil dot. Once this is done they can remove the mirror and draw a straight line between point P and the pencil dot.

8. Tell the same students to place the vertex of the *Angle Fixer* labeled "angle A" at point P and align the *mirror side* of the *Angle Fixer* with the mirror line. The *Angle Fixer* should "fit" the angle formed by the reflected pencil line and mirror line. Using the same *Angle Fixer*, tell the students to now compare the reflected angle to the angle labeled ∠1, the angle at which *Ray* struck the mirror, and record their comparison on their student pages.

9. Have different students repeat this process for positions B and C.

10. After all three positions have been tested, have the students develop a group response to question 2.

11. Have the students remove the mirrors from their student pages. Instruct them to place the *Angle Fixer* labeled "angle A" to the right side of point P with its vertex at point P and the side labeled "mirror side" aligned along the mirror line. Next, have them carefully add the angle B *Angle Fixer* to create a new angle. This angle equals angle A plus angle B. Ask them to mark this new angle with a pencil dot, remove the *Angle Fixers*, and draw the straight line connecting the dot to point P.

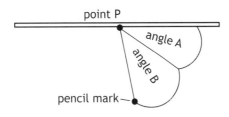

This line indicates a path *Rabbit Ray* reflects off the mirror, and travels along.

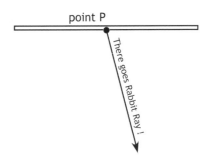

12. Challenge the students to draw the line *Rabbit Ray* must travel along in order to strike the mirror and reflect off along the line equal to angle A plus angle B.

Discussion

1. What do you know about *rays*. (Monitor their answers to be sure that at least these points are mentioned:
   - *ray* has a geometric meaning,
   - *ray* has a scientific meaning when used to describe the behavior of light energy,
   - a beam of light travels in a straight line unless it is reflected,
   - a light beam can be thought of as a bunch of light rays traveling in approximately the same direction,
   - the angle at which a light ray strikes a plane mirror equals the angle at which the light ray is reflected from the mirror,
   - and the *law of reflection* allows us to *predict* the behavior of reflected light rays.)

2. What is the relationship between the angle Rabbit Ray strikes the mirror and the angle Rabbit Ray reflects off the mirror? [The *angle of incidence* (the angle formed by the mirror and the illustrated line) equals the *angle of reflection* (the angle formed by the mirror and the *There goes Rabbit Ray!* line).]

3. How did you solve the *challenge* problem? Determine how many students *worked backwards* by directing a beam of light along the pencil line, towards the mirror, marking the position of the reflected beam. Find out if any students used the *Angle Fixers* to construct angle A plus angle B on the left side of point P, drew the *Here comes Rabbit Ray line!* and then checked their solution with their flashlight.

Extension: Teacher Demonstration Only

If a laser pointer is available, demonstrate for students how narrowing the light beam improves the accuracy at which the incident ray and the reflected ray can be compared.

* Reprinted with permission from *Principles and Standards for School Mathematics,* 2000 by the National Council of Teachers of Mathematics. All rights reserved.

Slit Stand Patterns

© 2000 AIMS Education Foundation

Likely Reflections

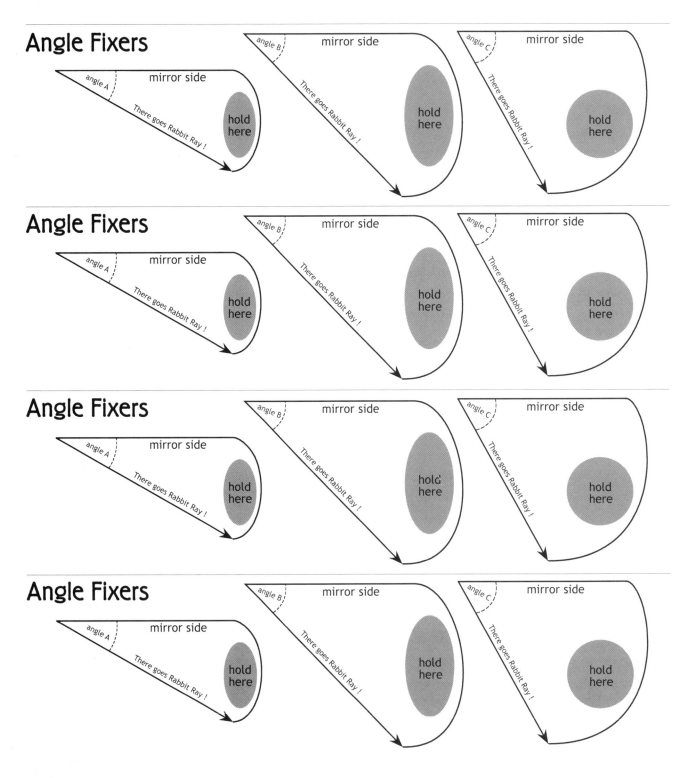

Angle Fixers

angle A · mirror side · There goes Rabbit Ray ! · hold here

angle B · mirror side · There goes Rabbit Ray ! · hold here

angle C · mirror side · There goes Rabbit Ray ! · hold here

Angle Fixers

angle A · mirror side · There goes Rabbit Ray ! · hold here

angle B · mirror side · There goes Rabbit Ray ! · hold here

angle C · mirror side · There goes Rabbit Ray ! · hold here

Angle Fixers

angle A · mirror side · There goes Rabbit Ray ! · hold here

angle B · mirror side · There goes Rabbit Ray ! · hold here

angle C · mirror side · There goes Rabbit Ray ! · hold here

Angle Fixers

angle A · mirror side · There goes Rabbit Ray ! · hold here

angle B · mirror side · There goes Rabbit Ray ! · hold here

angle C · mirror side · There goes Rabbit Ray ! · hold here

Likely Reflections

1. Compare angle A to ∠ 1 _____
   Compare angle B to ∠ 2 _____
   Compare angle C to ∠ 3 _____

2. In your own words, state the relationship between the angle Rabbit Ray strikes the mirror and the angle Rabbit Ray reflects off the mirror. (Use the back of this paper.)

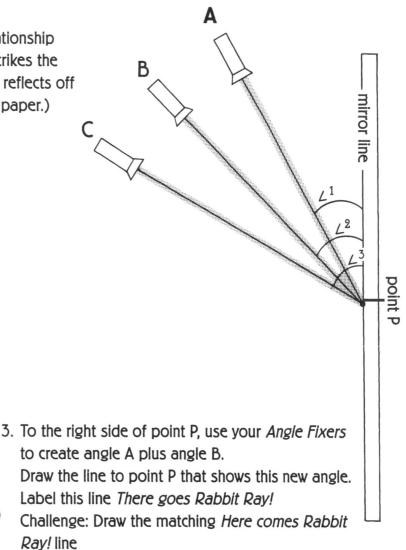

3. To the right side of point P, use your *Angle Fixers* to create angle A plus angle B.
   Draw the line to point P that shows this new angle.
   Label this line *There goes Rabbit Ray!*
   Challenge: Draw the matching *Here comes Rabbit Ray!* line

Second Sight

Topic
Plane mirror reflection

Key Question
What is the relationship between the angle at which a line of objects strikes a plane mirror and the angle at which the line of objects is reflected?

Focus
Students will align Rabbit Ray figures and observe that the angle at which a straight row of figures strikes a plane mirror equals the angle at which the images appear to leave the mirror.

Guiding Documents
Project 2061 Benchmark
* *...Something can be "seen" when light waves emitted or reflected by it enter the eye...*

NRC Standards
* *Light travels in a straight line until it strikes an object. Light can be reflected by a mirror, refracted by a lens, or absorbed by the object.*
* *Light interacts with matter by transmission (including refraction), absorption, or scattering (including reflection). To see an object, light from the object—emitted by or scattered from it—must enter the eye.*

NCTM Standards 2000*
* *Recognize geometric ideas and relationships and apply them to other disciplines and to problems that arise in the classroom or in everyday life*
* *Understand such attributes as length, area, weight, volume, and size of angle and select the appropriate type of unit for measuring each attribute*

Math
Measurement
    angle
Geometry and spatial sense

Science
Physical science
    light energy
        law of reflection

Integrated Processes
Observing
Inferring

Materials
For each pair of students:
    3" x 5" mirror
    binder clip for mirror support
    6 *Rabbit Ray Stand-up Figures*
    centimeter ruler

Background Information
The *law of reflection* for plane mirrors states that the angle of the incident (incoming) light ray is equal to angle of the reflected ray. In science texts, both the incident and reflected angles are usually measured from a line—called the *normal*—perpendicular to the surface of the mirror. The use of the normal makes reflection from *curved* surfaces easier to define.

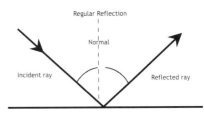

Students can *see* the reflecting surface—the mirror—but not the *normal line*. In this activity, the angles of incidence and reflection will be measured *from the mirror line*, not the normal line.

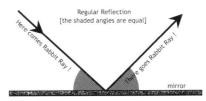

Management
1. To maximize instructional time, cut the left play field pages and glue or tape them to the right play field pages.

Make one play field for every two students. For repeated use, laminate the play fields.

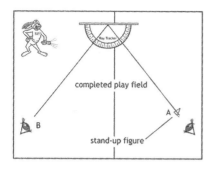

completed play field

stand-up figure

2. Make the *Rabbit Ray Stand-up Figures* before the activity or have students make their figures.
3. Organize the students into pairs.
4. Have one student color three of the Rabbit Ray figures one color and the other student the remaining three figures a different color.
5. Instruct the students to use the short vertical line at the base of each figure to align the figure.

Procedure

1. Have the students tape the play field to the top of a level table or desk.
2. Direct them to stand a 3" x 5" mirror at the position indicated on the play field.
3. Have one of the students start by placing one of the figures at the position labeled *A*. Tell the student to look in the direction indicated on the play field (at *A*). (The student will not see an image of the figure in the mirror.)
4. Have the second student then place one of the figures at the position labeled *B*. (This student will be able to see the image of the figure at *A* but not the image of his or her own figure at *B*.) Instruct the second student to position the figure at *B* so that it faces the image of the figure at *A*. (The first student can now see the image of the second student's figure in the mirror.)
5 Have the first student now place a second figure, as accurately as possible, in line with the images seen in the mirror.

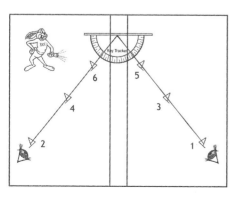

6. Direct the students to alternate turns, each placing a figure in line with the mirror image of the other student's line of figures.
7. To focus the student's observations, have the first student place a pencil over his/her line of figures. This simulates the *incident ray*. Have the second student place his/her eye so as to look over the lines of figures.
8. Instruct the first student to move the pencil towards the mirror. Have the second student observe, as the first student moves the pencil, the pencil coming towards them. This simulates the *reflected ray*.
9. Ask the students to change places and repeat this step.

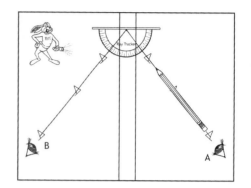

Discussion

1. How do the angles of incidence and the angles of reflection compare? [They are equal.]
2. Have students go back to the first step where the first student sets the figure. Why can the second student see the image of the first student's figure but the first student can't see the image of the figure? [The incident angle at which all of the light reflected off the figure, towards the mirror, has an angle of reflection that is always *away* from the eye of the first student.]

Extension

Have the first student select a location different from *A* and draw a pencil line from this position to the position labeled *O* at the mirror. Have the student place a figure on their side that lines up with the point labeled *O* and the image of the first student's figure. Tell them to use these new lines and repeat the experiment. Ask them to determine if the angle of incidence is equal to the angle of reflection for this different line.

* Reprinted with permission from *Principles and Standards for School Mathematics,* 2000 by the National Council of Teachers of Mathematics. All rights reserved.

Rabbit Ray Stand-up Figures

Instructions

1. Cut out the figure of Rabbit Ray along the solid lines.

2. Fold the sides of the figure along the dashed lines.

3. The figure can be easily positioned by grasping it along the folded edge.

4. This symbol represents the top view of a Stand-up Rabbit Ray figure.

Copy onto card stock.

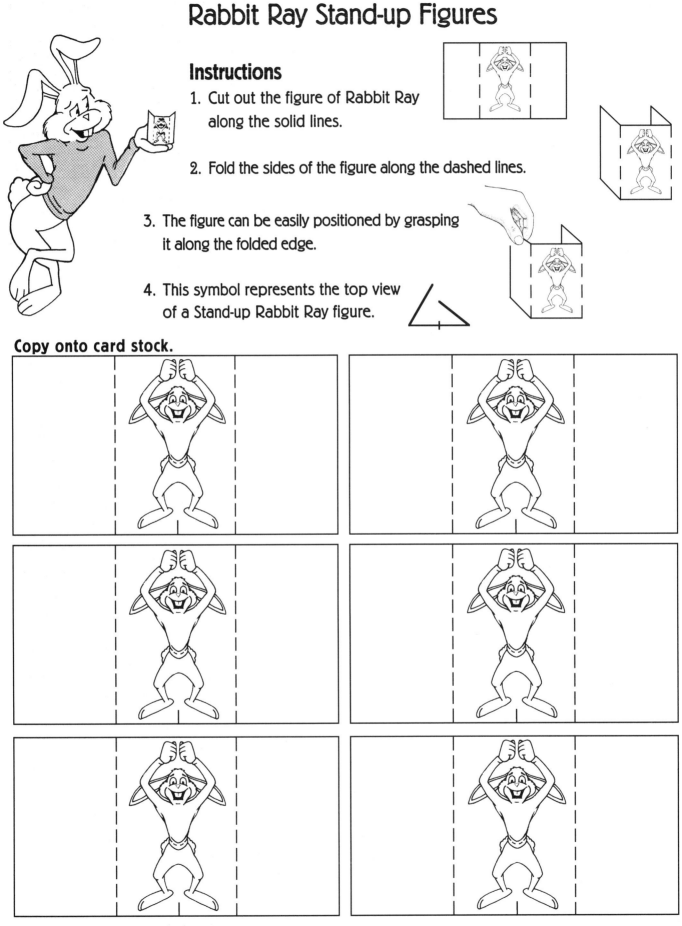

      © 2000 AIMS Education Foundation

Second Sight

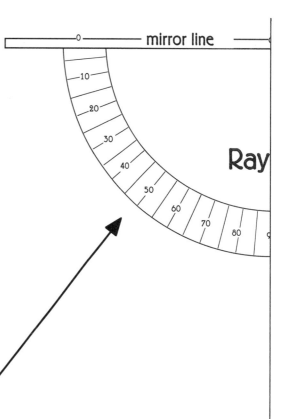

mirror line

—0—

—10—

—20—

—30—

—40—

—50—

—60—

—70—

—80—

9

Ray

B

cut along this line

2. Look in this direction. Stand a Rabbit Ray figure near the position labeled B. facing the image of the figure standing at A.

3. Alternate turns, each standing a Rabbit Ray figure in line with the mirror image of the other's line of Rabbit Ray figures.

© 2000 AIMS Education Foundation

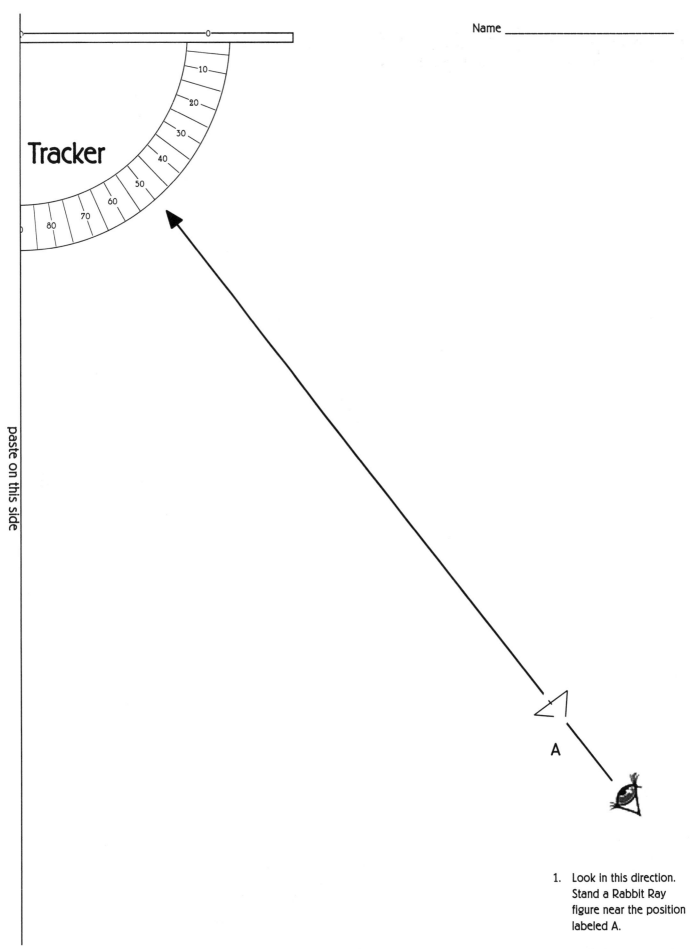

Name _____

Tracker

0

10
20
30
40
50
60
70
80

paste on this side

A

1. Look in this direction. Stand a Rabbit Ray figure near the position labeled A.

A Perplexing Parallel

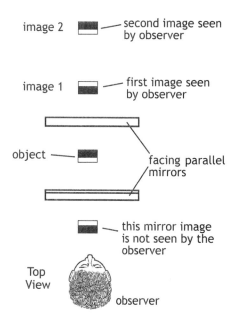

Topic
Plane mirror reflection

Key Question
How are the multiple images seen when an object is placed between parallel mirrors related to the actual object?

Focus
Students will explore the relationships between the multiple images seen when a figure is placed between two parallel mirrors. Students will trace the path the light follows to create each image.

Guiding Documents
Project 2061 Benchmark
- *…Something can be "seen" when light waves emitted or reflected by it enter the eye …*

NRC Standards
- *Light travels in a straight line until it strikes an object. Light can be reflected by a mirror, refracted by a lens, or absorbed by the object.*
- *Light interacts with matter by transmission (including refraction), absorption, or scattering (including reflection). To see an object, light from the object— emitted by or scattered from it—must enter the eye.*

NCTM Standard 2000*
- *Recognize geometric ideas and relationships and apply them to other disciplines and to problems that arise in the classroom or in everyday life*

Math
Measurement
 length

Science
Physical science
 light
  plane reflection

Integrated Processes
Observing
Generalizing
Applying
Predicting

Materials
For each pair of students:
 2 plane mirrors
 2 binder clips or blocks to support mirrors
 1 Reflect/View
 1 *Ray on a Stand* figure and 1 blank figure
 colored pencils or pens

Background Information
Multiple images of an object appear when the object is placed between two parallel, facing mirrors.

The unequally spaced images appear to recede along a line into the mirror. The receding images alternate as front and back images of the object placed between the mirrors.

To understand how the multiple images seen in two parallel mirrors are formed, you must do *Part One* and *Part Two* of this activity.

In the diagram, the first image the observer sees in the facing mirror is an image of the real object. Any real object would have two sides, a front and a back. In the diagram, the front of the object is shaded black. The second image seen by the observer is a reflection of the first image, unseen by this observer, formed in the mirror facing away from the observer. Note that the images of the front and back of the object alternate as they recede into the mirror.

By replacing both mirrors with a single Reflect/View and sketching the images as they appear in each mirror, one at a time, each student can explore the process by which these images are created.

Management

1. There are two parts to this activity. In *Part One* students observe the multiple images formed when an object is placed between two parallel, facing mirrors. In *Part Two* students use a mirror and a Reflect/View to analyze how the multiple images are formed.

2. Each pair of students needs to have access to two parallel mirrors and a Reflect/View to enable full participation.

3. It should be noted that when referring to the mirror images formed by facing parallel mirrors, each observer sees only the images visible in their mirror. These images will be labeled as *seen* images. Those images not actually visible to each observer will be labeled as *unseen* images.

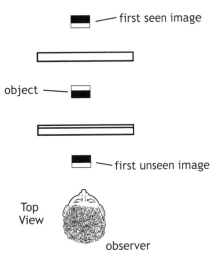

4. In *Part Two,* students will use a Reflect/View to locate a series of images. To assist students, faint guidelines for these locations are printed on the *Play Field 2* page.

Procedure

Part One: A Perplexing Parallel

1. Distribute a *Play Field 1* page to each pair of students. Instruct them to tape down the corners of the page so that each of the two students will be able to look over the top of one mirror.

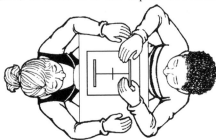

2. Tell the students to carefully place the mirrors, facing each other, at the locations printed on the page. Have them adjust the mirrors until the line on the page appears as a straight line in both mirrors.

3. Distribute a blank stand-up figure to each group.

4. Instruct the students to cut out and fold the blank figure to make a stand-up mountain.

Tell them to squeeze the sides of the mountain together and tape the bottom tabs at the location marked on the page. The figure is to face both mirrors.

5. Distribute the student page, *A Perplexing Parallel.* Tell the students to predict and record what they think they will see when they peek over the top of their mirror. Next, have them record what they actually did see.

6. Distribute one *Ray on a Stand* figure to each pair. Instruct the students to cut out and fold the figure to make a stand-up mountain. Tell them to color the front of Rabbit Ray's sweater one color and the back a different color. Have them tape the Rabbit Ray figure over the blank stand-up figure.

Again, ask them to predict what they think they will see when they peek over the top of their mirror.

7. Ask the students to record whether the first image they see in the mirror shows the front or back of Rabbit Ray.

8. Have the students compare their observations of the first mirror image each sees in their mirror.

9. Instruct the students to record how many of the images of Rabbit Ray are looking towards them.

10. Have the students record how many of the images are looking away from them.

Discussion

1. What did you predict you would see?
2. What did you actually see? [a line of images receding back into the mirror]
3. After coloring Rabbit Ray's sweater, what did you predict you would see?
4. What did you actually see? [a receding line of alternating (front, back, or back, front) images of Rabbit Ray]
5. What is the first image you see in your mirror? Is it Rabbit Ray's front or his back? [The *first* image any student sees in the mirror will be a reflection of the side of the *Ray on a Stand* figure facing *away* from them.]
6. In the receding line of Rabbit Ray images, how many are looking away from you? [half]
7. In the receding line of Rabbit Ray images, how many are looking at you? [half]
8. Do the images appear to be equally or unequally spaced? [unequally spaced]

Procedure

Part Two: How the Images are Formed

1. Distribute one Reflect/View to each group. Distribute a *Play Field 2* page and the *How the Multiple Images are Formed* pages to each student.
2. Have students follow the directions on the *How the Images are Formed* pages.

Discussion

1. How far is the first image seen in the mirror from the first mirror line? [1 unit]
2. What is the first image seen in the mirror an image of? [The rectangle that represents the Rabbit Ray figure.]
3. How far is the second image seen in the mirror from the first mirror line? [3 units]
4. What is the second image seen in the mirror an image of? [The first unseen image.] Why do you think it is called the unseen image? [When I look in a single mirror, I can't see it. I would need two mirrors to see it.]
5. How far is the third image seen in the mirror from the first mirror line? [5 units]
6. What is the third image seen in the mirror an image of? [the second unseen image]
7. What patterns did you discover? [The number of the seen images is one more than the number of the unseen images. The distance of the seen images from the mirror line is an odd number. The distance the image is from the mirror line is one less than twice the number of the image. For example, the third image is $(3 \times 2) - 1 = 5$ units from the mirror line. The front-back pattern alternates.]
8. What was your prediction for the fourth image seen in the mirror? [The fourth image seen in the

mirror is 7 units from the mirror line and is the reflection of the third unseen image. The fourth image will have the same front-back pattern as the second image.]
9. What method did you devise for testing your prediction?
10. How accurate was your prediction?

Extensions

1. If students are able to generalize, have them describe the nth image seen in the mirror. [The nth image is a reflection of the $(n-1)$ unseen image. The nth image is $(2n-1)$ units from the mirror line. All odd numbered images will have the front-back pattern of the first image. All even number images will have the front-back pattern of the second image.]
2. Extend the activity by exploring what would happen if the mirrors were parallel but not directly opposite each other. Place one mirror four units to the right.

   What does one see now?

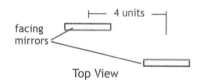

Top View

3. What is a real-world application of parallel mirrors? [The periscope. See the activity, *Ray's Around the Corner.*]

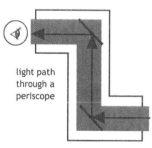

light path through a periscope

* Reprinted with permission from *Principles and Standards for School Mathematics,* 2000 by the National Council of Teachers of Mathematics. All rights reserved.

Rabbit Ray on a Stand

Instructions

1. Cut out and fold the blank figure to make a stand-up mountain.

2. Squeeze the sides of the mountain together and tape the bottom tabs at the location marked on the *Play Field 1* page.

3. *The Ray on a Stand* figure is cut, folded, and taped over the blank figure.

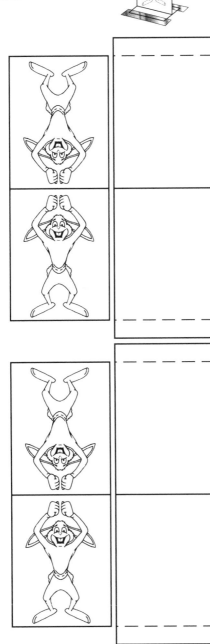
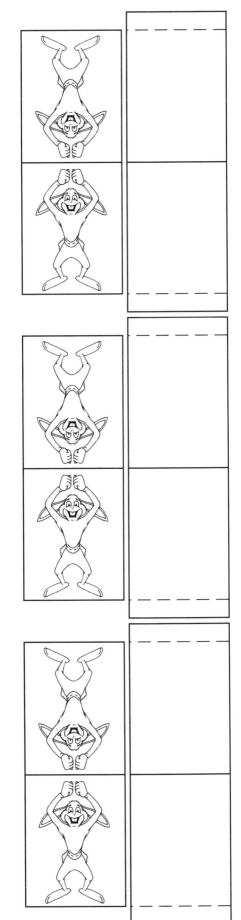

80

© 2000 AIMS Education Foundation

A Perplexing Parallel

Set up the two mirrors and the blank stand-up figure at the locations shown on the Play Field 1 page.

1. What will you see if you peek over the top of your mirror?
   I think I'll see:

   I saw:

Cut out a *Ray on a Stand* figure. Color the front of Rabbit Ray's sweater one color and the back of his sweater a different color. Fold and tape the *Ray on a Stand* figure over the blank figure.

2. What will you see in the mirror?
   Before looking, I think I'll see:

   I saw:

3. Record whether the first image you see in the mirror is the front or back of Rabbit Ray.

4. Compare your observation of your first mirror image with your partner's observation of his or her first image.

5. How many Rabbit Rays are looking away from you? (You can see the back of Rabbit Ray's sweater.)

6. How many Rabbit Rays are looking at you? (You can see the front of Rabbit Ray's sweater.)

7. Do the images appear to be equally or unequally spaced?

A Perplexing Parallel

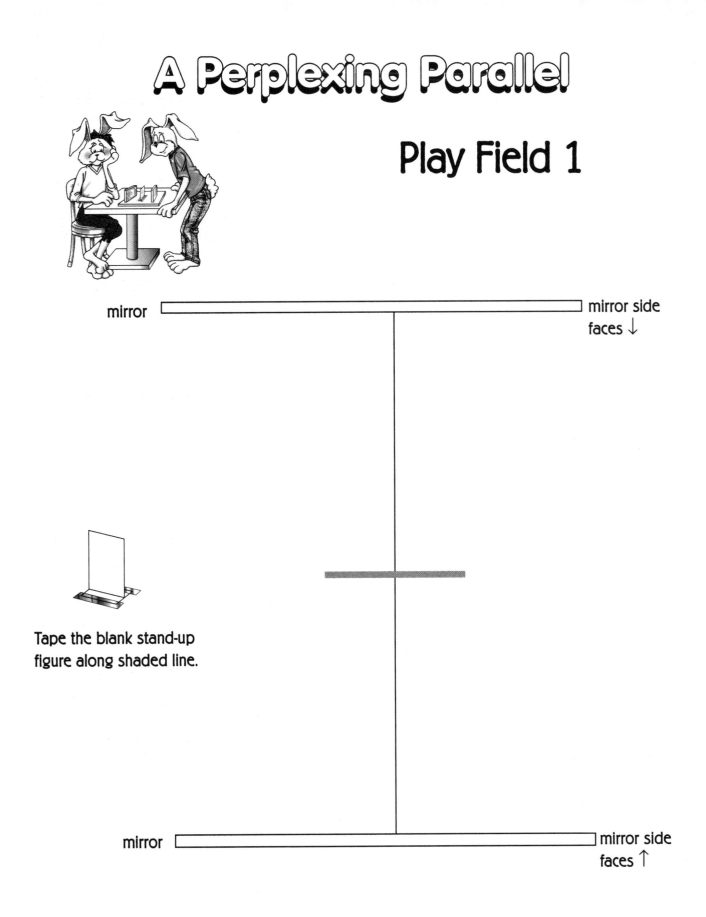

mirror

mirror side
faces ↓

Tape the blank stand-up
figure along shaded line.

mirror

mirror side
faces ↑

© 2000 AIMS Education Foundation

A Perplexing Parallel
How the Multiple Images are Formed
Play Field 2

When looking over the top of one of the two parallel mirrors, you see a line of images going back, into the mirror. How are these images formed? Part of the answer lies in locating the images you don't see when peeking over the top of one of the mirrors. Follow these steps to help you answer the question.

Step 1.   Tape down the corners of your Play Field 2 page. Color the rectangle on Play Field 2 as you colored the front and back of Rabbit Ray's sweater on Play Field 1.

front or back of Rabbit Ray's sweater — the opposite side of Rabbit Ray's sweater

To observe the first image you see in the mirror, place a mirror on the first mirror line and look into the mirror.

To accurately draw the location of this image, replace the mirror with a Reflect/View. Look through the Reflect/View and draw the reflected image onto the image line.

Color the drawn image, record its distance from the first mirror line, and the source of the image.

Step 2.   Place a mirror on the dashed line labeled second mirror line. Looking from the top of the page towards the bottom of the page, observe the first image in the mirror.

To accurately draw the location of this image, replace the mirror with a Reflect/View. Looking from the top of the page towards the bottom of the page, look through the Reflect/View and draw the first reflected image onto the image line.

Since this image is not seen when looking into the mirror, record this image as the first unseen image. Color the drawn image.

Step 3.   Place a mirror back on the first mirror line. Looking from the bottom of the page towards the top, observe the second image seen in the mirror. Put your finger on the first unseen image you drew and observe that it's the second image in the mirror.

To accurately draw the location of this image, replace the mirror with a Reflect/View. Look through the Reflect/View and draw the second reflected image onto the image line. Color the drawn image, record its distance from the first mirror line, and the source of the image.

Step 4. Place a mirror back on the second mirror line. Looking from the top of the page towards the bottom, observe the second image seen in the mirror.

To accurately draw the location of this image, replace the mirror with a Reflect/View. Look through the Reflect/View and draw the second reflected image onto the image line. Color the drawn image. Record this image as the second unseen image.

Step 5. Place a mirror back on the first mirror line. Looking from the bottom of the page towards the top, observe the third image seen in the mirror. Put your finger on the second unseen image you drew and observe that it's the third image in the mirror.

To accurately draw the location of this image, replace the mirror with a Reflect/View. Look through the Reflect/View and draw the second reflected image onto the image line. Color the drawn image. Record this image as the second unseen image.

Step 6. Look for a pattern in the data recorded on Play Field 2 and use your findings to predict the data for the fourth image seen in the mirror.

(color in)

Prediction:
The fourth image seen in the mirror is _____ units from the mirror line and is the reflection of the _____ image in the opposite mirror.

The color pattern for the rectangle is:

Step 7. Devise a method for testing your prediction.

Explain your method for testing your prediction.

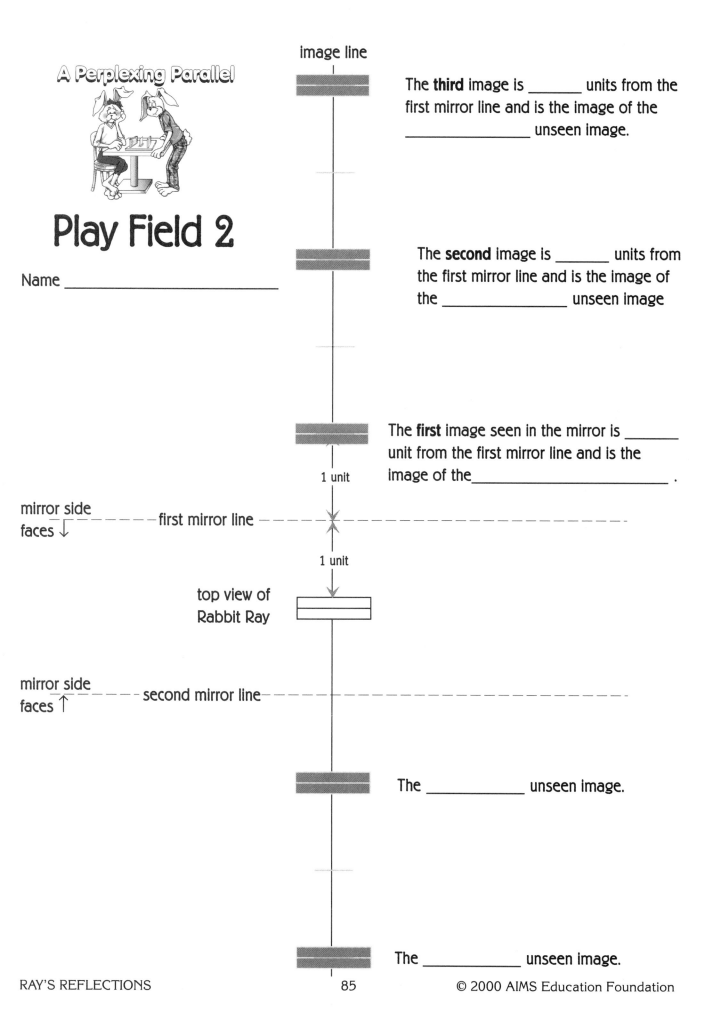

A Perplexing Parallel

Play Field 2

Name _____

image line

The **third** image is _____ units from the first mirror line and is the image of the _____ unseen image.

The **second** image is _____ units from the first mirror line and is the image of the _____ unseen image

The **first** image seen in the mirror is _____ unit from the first mirror line and is the image of the_____ .

1 unit

mirror side faces ↓ — — first mirror line — — — — — — — — — — — — — — — —

1 unit

top view of Rabbit Ray

mirror side faces ↑ — — second mirror line — — — — — — — — — — — — — — —

The _____ unseen image.

The _____ unseen image.

© 2000 AIMS Education Foundation

HOORAY FOR RABBIT RAY!

Topic
Plane mirror reflection

Key Questions
1. How can you position two pencil poles, one in front of a plane mirror, the other in a fixed position behind the mirror, so that the image in the mirror lines up with the pole *behind the mirror, along any line of sight,* when viewed from in front of the mirror?
2. What's the relationship between the line of sight of two pencil poles, one placed in front of a plane mirror, the other fixed in place behind the mirror, and the line between the *image in the mirror* and the object placed behind the mirror?

Focus
Students will have an opportunity to apply the relationship—*perpendicular to and equal distance from*—between an object and its reflection in a plane mirror.

Guiding Documents
Project 2061 Benchmark
• *...Something can be "seen" when light waves emitted or reflected by it enter the eye...*

NRC Standards
• *Light travels in a straight line until it strikes an object. Light can be reflected by a mirror, refracted by a lens, or absorbed by the object.*
• *Light interacts with matter by transmission (including refraction), absorption, or scattering (including reflection). To see an object, light from the object—emitted by or scattered from it—must enter the eye.*

NCTM Standards 2000*
• *Recognize geometric ideas and relationships and apply them to other disciplines and to problems that arise in the classroom or in everyday life*
• *Understand such attributes as length, area, weight, volume, and size of angle and select the appropriate type of unit for measuring each attribute*
• *Solve problems that arise in mathematics and in other contexts*

Math
Geometry and spatial sense
    line segment
    perpendicular

Science
Physical science
    light
        plane reflection

Integrated Processes
Observing
Comparing and contrasting
Applying

Materials
For each group:
    1 *Rabbit Ray Statue and Pole*
    plane mirror
    binder clip for mirror support

Background Information
Even though students have done several "perpendicular to and equidistant from" mirror activities, it may still be difficult to think about reflection in a plane mirror. In this activity the position of the "mirror image" is given and the student is asked to place the object, Ray's statue, so the statue and its mirror image coincide.

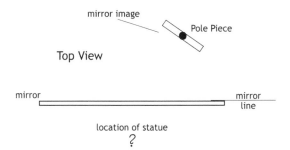

Typically, students use a trial and error approach to locate the position in front of the mirrored wall to place Ray's statue, not the "perpendicular to and equidistant from" relationship. Trial and error can quickly establish a position that solves the problem, from a *single point of view*, but only the "perpendicular

© 2000 AIMS Education Foundation

to and equidistant from" relationship gives the correct location for *all points of view.*

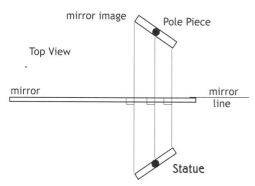

mirror image   Pole Piece

Top View

mirror   mirror
line

Statue

A learner using the "perpendicular to and equidistant from" relationship would be seen sketching perpendicular lines on the student page as guidelines for placing Ray's statue.

This activity is a good assessment of a student's understanding of the "perpendicular to and equidistant from" relationship for plane mirrors.

Management
1. Set the stage for this activity. Tell students that the plane mirror activities they have already done should help them succeed in this activity.
2. Make the Rabbit Ray statues and pole pieces before the activity or have students make them. There are two sets of statues and poles per page.
3. Be sure you do the activity yourself before asking students to do it. To be in the position to best help your students, it's necessary for you to experience the problem.

Procedure
1. Distribute the materials.
2. Instruct the students to place the pole piece at the position marked on their student sheets. Tell them to align the mark at the base of their pole piece with the center of the spot on their sheet. This pole piece remains fixed.
3. Read this to the class:

A Tribute to Rabbit Ray
Light is so important that a local mall has decided to erect a statue to Rabbit Ray in its central courtyard.

When told of this, Rabbit Ray suggested that two statues could be had for little more than the price of one.

His idea is to pay a sculptor for a single statue, put the sculpture in front of a mirrored wall, and thereby have two statues visible to shoppers.

When shown where his statue was to be placed, Rabbit Ray noticed a large floor to ceiling pole that would be behind the mirrored wall, once the wall was built. Rabbit Ray

thought a minute, and then said, "Add a pole to my statue and there is one spot, but just one spot, where the image of my statue will merge with the pole behind the wall. With my statue placed at this spot, both the statue and its image will look natural from any position in the courtyard."

Where is this location?

4. Tell the students to place their Rabbit Ray statue in front of the mirror. Instruct them to find the eye position where the part of the pole piece behind the mirror (but visible over the top of the mirror) just matches the image of the pole of Rabbit Ray's statue located in front of the mirror.
5. Ask the *Key Question:* Where can you position Rabbit Ray's statue so that its mirror image is aligned with the statue pole when viewed from any eye position in front of the mirror?
6. Give students time to manipulate their poles and answer the question.
7. Once students think they have the answer, ask them to complete their activity sheet.

Discussion
1. Compared to previous activities, what was new about this activity?
2. Compared to previous activities, what was the same about this activity?
3. Have the students sketch the "perpendicular to and equidistant from" relationship (see illustration) on their student page.

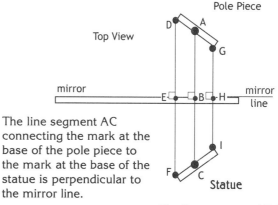

Pole Piece

Top View

mirror   mirror
line

Statue

The line segment AC connecting the mark at the base of the pole piece to the mark at the base of the statue is perpendicular to the mirror line.

The line segment AB is equal to the line segment BC.

4. Discuss the relative merits of the trial and error versus the "perpendicular to and equidistant from" relationship for solving the problem.

* Reprinted with permission from *Principles and Standards for School Mathematics,* 2000 by the National Council of Teachers of Mathematics. All rights reserved.

© 2000 AIMS Education Foundation

HOORAY FOR RABBIT RAY!

Rabbit Ray Statue and Pole

1. Cut out each Rabbit Ray Statue and Pole piece along the dark lines.

2. Fold the sides of each piece to the back along the dashed lines.

3. Stand each piece and trim the base if needed.

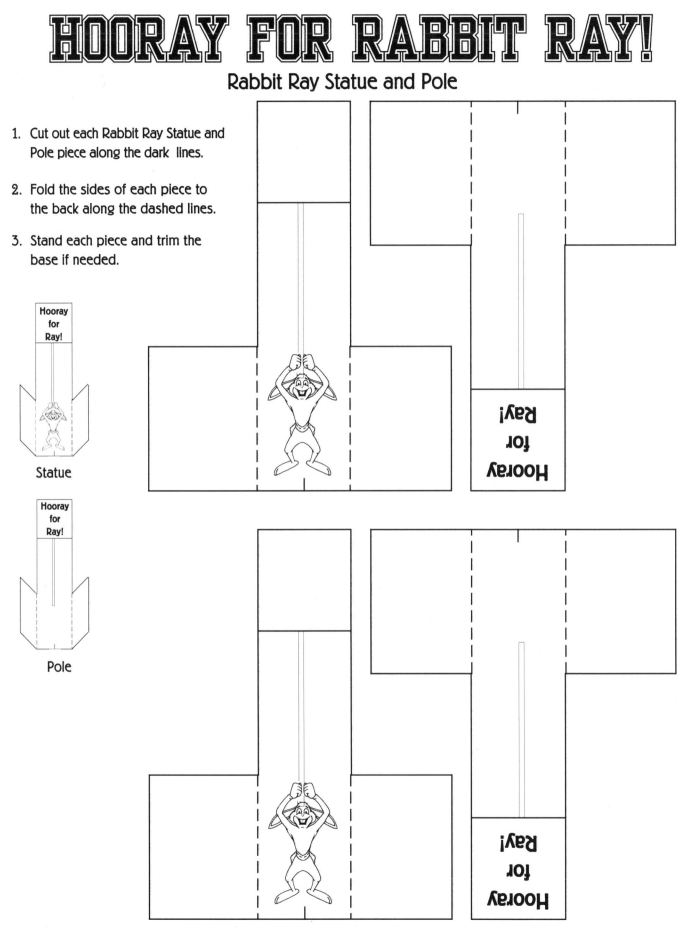

Statue

Pole

Hooray for Ray!

HOORAY FOR RABBIT RAY!

A statue is going to be erected to Rabbit Ray.

There is a floor-to-ceiling pole on one side an eight-foot high wall.

Ray's statue will be placed on the other side of the wall. That side of the wall is mirrored. A reflection of Ray's statue will be seen in the mirrored wall.

Where should Rabbit Ray's statue be placed so that, from every possible position in front of the mirrored wall, the reflection of the statue, as seen in the mirrored wall, will always match the pole and sign behind the wall? This creates the illusion of two complete statues as viewed from in front of the mirrored wall.

Build a model to test your solution. To set up your model, stand a mirror upright at the position indicated. Place only a pole at the position labeled "Fixed Pole." Place Rabbit Ray's statue in front of the mirror so that it appears there are two perfectly matched statues.

Top View of the Courtyard at the Mall

Fixed Pole

Place the pole at the indicated position.

mirror line   stand the mirror here   Mirror Wall

Where, on this side of the mirror, should you place Rabbit Ray's statue? Mark the position of the statue.

Topic
Plane mirror reflection and line symmetry

Key Question
How is plane mirror reflection related to line symmetry?

Focus
Students will use a Reflect/View to place the reflected image of a hat onto the head of Rabbit Ray. Students will discover that the line along which the mirror is placed to reflect the hat onto the head is a *line of symmetry*.

Guiding Documents
Project 2061 Benchmark
- *Symmetry can be found by reflection, turns, or slides.*

NCTM Standards 2000*
- *Recognize geometric ideas and relationships and apply them to other disciplines and to problems that arise in the classroom or in everyday life*
- *Describe sizes, positions, and orientations of shapes under informal transformations such as flips, turns, slides, and scaling*

Math
Measurement
    length
Geometry and spatial sense
    line symmetry

Science
Physical science
    light
        plane reflection

Integrated Processes
Observing
Comparing and contrasting
Generalizing

Materials
1 Reflect/View for each group of two students

Background Information
    The similarity between the science concept of a *light ray* and the mathematical concept of a *geometrical ray* is an excellent example of the integration of science and mathematics. In *optics*, the branch of physics that studies the behavior of light, the geometrical ray becomes the mathematical model for the physical light ray.

    The mathematical concept of *line symmetry* is used in science to explain how images are formed in plane mirrors. To go from the mathematical context to the science context, one simply needs to stand a plane mirror vertically along the line of symmetry. Every point on the reflected image is related to every point on the object being reflected by the "equal to" and "perpendicular to" relationships that define line symmetry.

Principles of Plane Mirror Reflection
For a plane mirror, the line connecting any object and its mirror image is perpendicular (normal) to the mirror, and the object and image are equidistant from the mirror.

    Points *A* and *C* are symmetric with respect to line *L* if, and only if, line *L* perpendicularly bisects the line segment joining the points *A* and *C*.

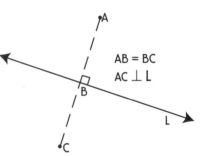

    If a plane mirror is placed vertically along line *L* then the image of point *C*, as seen in the mirror, appears at point *A*.

    A geometric figure is symmetric with respect to a line if, and only if, every point on the figure on one side of the line is matched by a symmetrical point on the opposite side of the line.

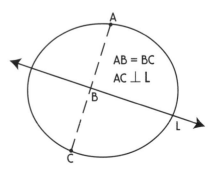

This activity gives students the opportunity to explore line symmetry in both the mathematical and the science contexts. In the activity, students are asked to reflect hats onto Rabbit Ray's head. To do so, students must locate the line of symmetry between the hat and the rabbit so that when the image of the hat is viewed through a Reflect/View, the image is superimposed onto the rabbit's head.

The student is first allowed to use the trial-and-error method to place each hat on the rabbit's head.

Management

1. The first student page, *Ray's Hat Rack*, lets students explore the relationship between plane mirror reflection and the mathematical concept of line symmetry. The second student page, *Crossing the Line,* directly connects plane mirror reflection to the mathematical concept of line symmetry. *Ray's Challenge*, the third student page, allows students to assess their understanding of the relationship between plane mirror reflection and line symmetry.
2. Work through all three pages and decide which pages will help your students meet the science and mathematics learning objectives you've set for them.

Procedure
Ray's Hat Rack
1. Distribute one *Ray's Hat Rack* page to each student.
2. Instruct students to pick any one of the hats and place their Reflect/Views between the hat and the rabbit. Tell them to look through the Reflect/View, from the hat side, and move the Reflect/View until the image of the hat appears to be on the rabbit's head. Allow students sufficient time to repeat the process for each of the five hats.

Discussion
Students will typically be so excited putting the hats on Ray's head that they will notice little else about the relationship between the hat, the image of the hat, and Ray. Throughout the discussion phase of the activity, students should have their Reflect/Views and activity pages handy so they can quickly and easily make any observations raised by the discussion.
1. What is the difference between looking through the Reflect/View from the hat side and looking through the Reflect/View from the rabbit's side? [When viewing from the hat's side, the hat is reflected onto the rabbit. Viewing from the rabbit's side, Ray is reflected onto the hat.]
2. What number is printed on the firefighter's helmet. [At first glance, the number on the fire hat printed on the page appears to be "71" but turning the page reveals that the "7" is backwards. The number seen on the *image* of the hat is "17."]
3. Notice the small shaded dot on each hat. Describe the relationship between the dot on the hat and the

image of the dot and hat. [The printed dot is on the opposite side of the hat from the *image* dot.] Darken each dot to make this reversal easier to see.

Procedure
Crossing the Line
1. Distribute one *Crossing the Line* page to every student.
2. Use the upper left box containing Rabbit Ray and the fire hat to explain the principle of line symmetry. Instruct students to place their Reflect/View on the line of symmetry between Ray and the fire hat and verify that line segments AE = CE and BF = DF.

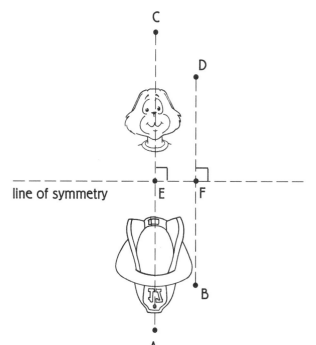

3. Tell students to follow the instructions contained in the first box and complete the page.

Discussion
1. Compare the line-of-symmetry method you used to put the hat on Ray with the method you used on the first page, the trial-and-error method. [The line-of-symmetry method requires us to *think* about the geometric and mathematical relationships between Ray and the hat. The trial-and-error method is a visual feedback process much like steering a bicycle or car; you look at where you are, where you want to go, and then make left-right changes to correct direction errors. You don't have to know any mathematics to do this, so it's easier.]
2. What creative people can you think of that need to know the mathematics of light reflection? [Artists and the people that work on special effects for television and the movies have to know the mathematics of reflection whenever they need to program their

computers to create any effects that use mirrors or other surfaces to reflect light.]

3. Explain why the shaded dot on each hat was helpful. [The one dot helped establish the location of the line of symmetry. If a second dot were placed on the hat, it helped establish the *direction* of the line of symmetry.]

Procedure
Ray's Challenge

1. Tell the students to put aside their Reflect/Views. Inform them that they are not allowed to use their Reflect/Views for this activity.
2. Distribute one *Ray's Challenge* page to every student.
3. Challenge them to first estimate and then draw the position of the line of symmetry and then to draw the image of the hat on the Ray's head as it would look when seen through a Reflect/View.

Discussion

1. How can you check the accuracy of your line of symmetry? [Using the Reflect/View, we can determine the accuracy of our line of symmetry estimation by how close the image of the hat is to being on the rabbit's head. We can compare our drawing of the hat's image with the reflected image to judge how accurately we estimated the reflected image.]
2. Tell students to once again put away their Reflect/Views and to look at their pages. Tell them you're going to ask a question and give them only 30 seconds to think. Looking from the hat side of the Reflect/View, does the bill of the hat point to Ray's left or right? [his left]
3. Looking from the rabbit's side of the Reflect/View, does the hat bill point to Ray's left or right? [his right] Explain why.

* Reprinted with permission from *Principles and Standards for School Mathematics*, 2000 by the National Council of Teachers of Mathematics. All rights reserved.

A Hat Trick: Ray's Hat Rack

Rabbit Ray has several different hats hanging on the hat rack.
Place your Reflect/View between each hat and Ray so that each of the hats is reflected onto his head.

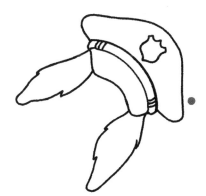

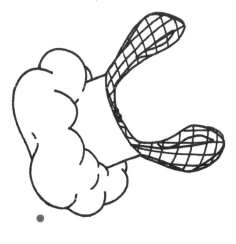

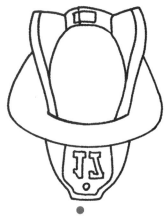

© 2000 AIMS Education Foundation

1. Mark two separate points, A and B, on Ray's hat.
2. Mark the points C and D you predict points A and B will be reflected to.
3. Sketch the line of symmetry that will reflect the two points.
4. Check your prediction with your Reflect/View.

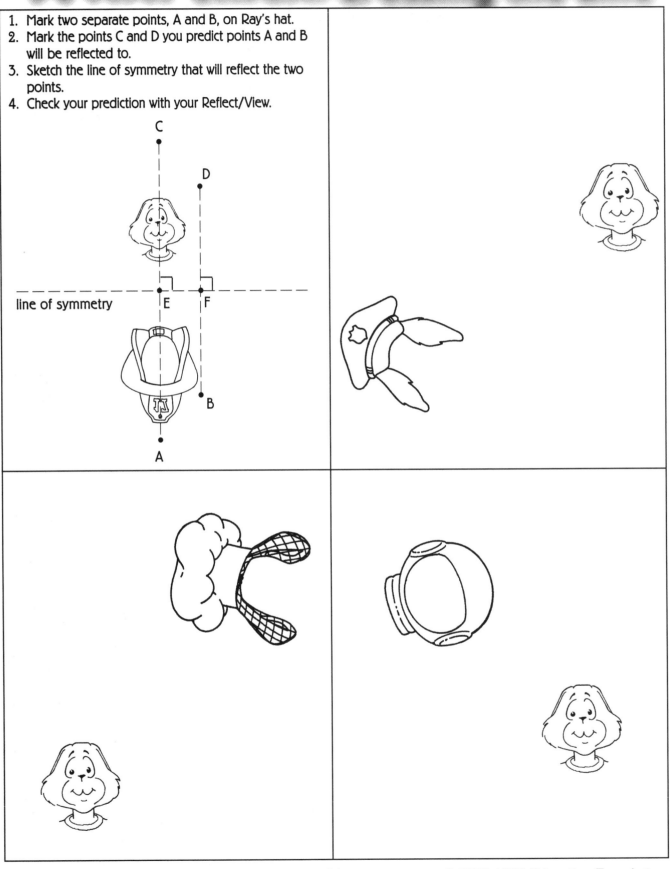

line of symmetry

A Hat Trick:
Ray's Challenge

1. Ray challenges you to draw the line of symmetry—without using your Reflect/View—that will reflect his baseball hat onto his head.

2. He asks that you draw the image of his hat onto his head as you would see the hat if it were reflected along the line of symmetry you drew.

3. Check your solution by placing a Reflect/View on the line of symmetry you drew.

Open and Shut

Topic
Plane reflection
 multiple images

Key Question
What is the relationship between the number of images seen within a hinged mirror and the acute angle formed at the hinge?

Focus
Students will use a hinged mirror to explore the multiple reflections of an image. Students will establish the mathematical relationship between the angle formed by the hinged mirror and the number of images seen in the hinged mirror.

Guiding Documents
Project 2061 Benchmark
- *…Something can be "seen" when light waves emitted or reflected by it enter the eye…*

NRC Standards
- *Light travels in a straight line until it strikes an object. Light can be reflected by a mirror, refracted by a lens, or absorbed by the object.*
- *Light interacts with matter by transmission (including refraction), absorption, or scattering (including reflection). To see an object, light from the object—emitted by or scattered from it—must enter the eye.*

NCTM Standards 2000*
- *Use geometric models to solve problems in other areas of mathematics, such as number and measurement*
- *Recognize geometric ideas and relationships and apply them to other disciplines and to problems that arise in the classroom or in everyday life*
- *Select and apply appropriate standard units and tools to measure length, area, volume, weight, time, temperature, and the size of angles*

Math
Geometry and spatial sense
 measuring angles

Science
Physical science
 plane reflection
  multiple images of a point-like object

Integrated Processes
Observing
Predicting
Collecting and organizing data
Inferring
Generalizing

Materials
Mirrors
Protractors

Background Information
When two plane mirrors are taped together along an edge to form a *hinged mirror*, multiple images of an object can be seen. For example, if the angle between the mirror surfaces is 60 degrees, two images of an object can be seen in the mirrors. For simplicity, if we call the object itself an image, then we can say we see three images.

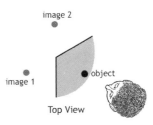

Top View

As the angle between the two mirrors is increased or decreased, the number of images seen also increases or decreases. If the angle equals 90 degrees, four images can be seen.

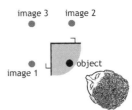

If the angle equals 72 degrees, five images are visible.

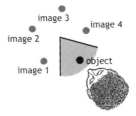

 © 2000 AIMS Education Foundation

Counting the reflected object as an image, the relationship between the number of images seen and the angle between the two mirrors is

mirror angle x number of images seen = 360°

In this activity students explore the multiple images created with a hinged mirror. Next, they will establish the fundamental relationship between the angle at the hinge and the number of images seen.

Management
1. Hinged mirrors can be purchased from AIMS or sheets of mirrored glass (approximately 8" x 11") can be purchased inexpensively at any department-type store or hardware outlet. Cut with a glass cutter into desired lengths (approximately 3" x 5") and tape the edges with masking tape for safety in handling. To make the hinge, place two mirrors, reflective side down, with two 3" sides nearly abutting. Tape across the backs of the two mirrors to join them together.
2. Have students work in teams of two or three, depending upon the number of mirrors available.
3. If protractors are not available, make transparencies of the *Rabbit Ray's Protractor* page and make as many student protractors as needed.

Procedure
1. Show a hinged mirror to the students. Name the parts of the mirror for the students and compare the hinged mirror to a geometric angle.

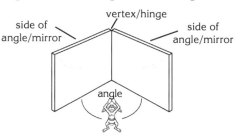

2. Distribute the *Exploring a Hinged Mirror* student page.
3. Instruct the students to stand the hinged mirror on the page and place the vertex of the mirror on the small circle labeled *hinge*.
4. Tell the students to look into the hinged mirror and, without moving the hinge off the circle, open and close the mirror.
5. Allow students time to discover and explore the fact that increasing or decreasing the angle increases or decreases the number of images seen in the hinged mirror.
6. Ask students to describe the *general* relationship between the angle and the number of images.

Discussion
1. Describe the relationship between the angle at the hinge and the number of images you saw. [Increasing the angle *decreases* the number of images, decreasing the angle *increases* the number of images.]

Procedure
1. Distribute the *Angles and Images* page.
2. Instruct the students to look at *Figure A* and record their prediction for the number of images (counting Ray himself) they think they will see when they place a hinged mirror on the figure. Tell them to repeat this step for *Figures B–E*.
3. Direct the students to place their hinged mirrors on the dashed lines above the picture of Rabbit Ray in *Figure A*.
4. Instruct them to look into the mirror and count and record the number of images (including Ray himself) they see.
5. Have them repeat this step for *Figures B–E*.

Discussion
1. How did your predictions compare to the actual count?
2. What did you learn by using the hinged mirror that would have helped you make better predictions?

Procedure
1. Distribute the *Ray's Protractor Practice* page.
2. Review with students the procedure for using a protractor to measure an angle.
3. Direct the students to measure and record the angle measure for each of the angles in *Figures A–E*.
4. Tell them to look at their *Angles and Images* page and copy into the table their prediction and the actual count for *Figures A–E*.
5. Ask the students to look for a pattern in the table and then describe the relationship between the number of degrees in the angle formed by the hinged mirror and the number of images seen in the mirror.

Discussion
1. How is the angle related to the number of images? [The mirror angle x number of images = 360°.]
2. What other patterns did you notice? [As the angle measure increases, the number of images decreases, and vice versa.]

Procedure

1. Distribute the *Check It Out!* page.
2. Instruct the students to use the relationship they discovered in *Angle and Images* to predict the number of star images they should see for each angle listed in the table.
3. Tell the students to check their predictions by placing their hinged mirrors on the 30°, 20°, 15°, and 10° lines printed on the protractor.

Discussion

1. For the 30° angle, compare your prediction to the actual count. [360°/30 = 12, the 12 images are easily seen and counted]
2. Why were you able to count only 17 images at the 20° angle? How many did you expect to be able to count? [The ninth image is hidden behind the hinge.]

3. How did your prediction compare to the actual count at the 15° and 10° angles? [It is difficult, but not impossible to count the correct number of images at the 15° lines. Leaning back from the mirror helps. Also, the twelfth image is hidden behind the hinge. At the 10° lines, the images near the hinge blur together making counting difficult and inaccurate.]
4. In applying what you've learned about multiple mirrors and images, how many images do you think you can produce with two mirrors? [As the angle approaches zero, the number of images approaches infinity.]

*   Reprinted with permission from *Principles and Standards for School Mathematics,* 2000 by the National Council of Teachers of Mathematics. All rights reserved.

© 2000 AIMS Education Foundation

Open and Shut
EXPLORING A HINGED MIRROR

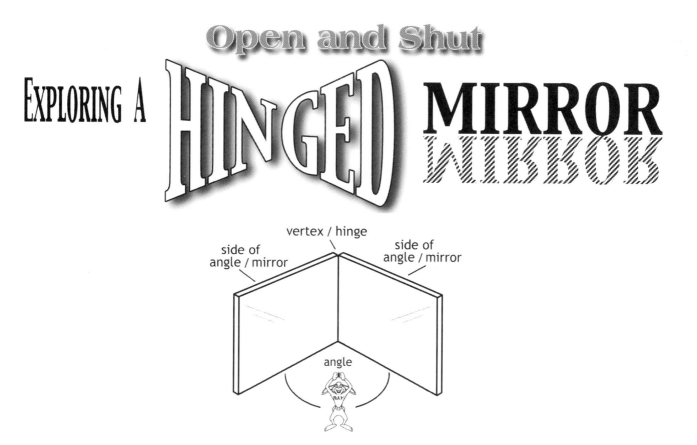

Stand your hinged mirror at the location shown below (be sure the hinge is on the circle labeled hinge). To explore, look into the hinged mirror and open and close the sides of the mirror.

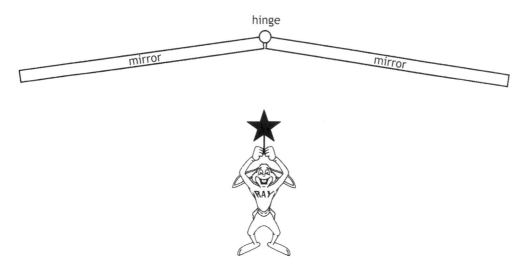

What is the general relationship between the angle and the number of images you see in the hinged mirror?

Open and Shut

Angles and IMAGES

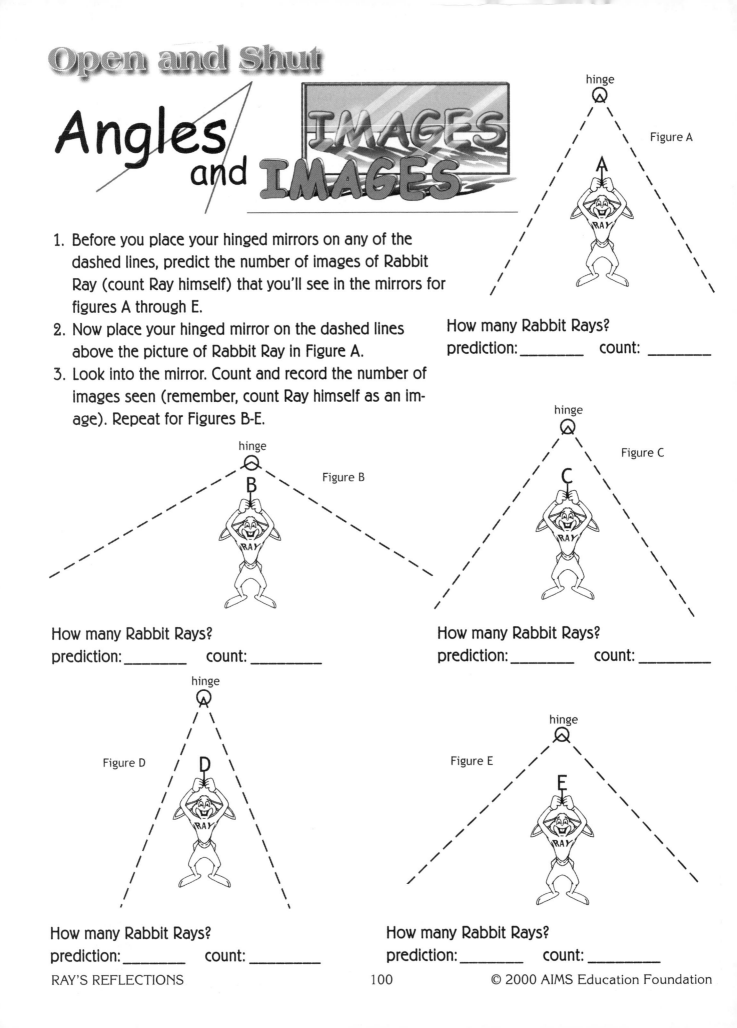

1. Before you place your hinged mirrors on any of the dashed lines, predict the number of images of Rabbit Ray (count Ray himself) that you'll see in the mirrors for figures A through E.

2. Now place your hinged mirror on the dashed lines above the picture of Rabbit Ray in Figure A.

3. Look into the mirror. Count and record the number of images seen (remember, count Ray himself as an image). Repeat for Figures B-E.

hinge

Figure A

How many Rabbit Rays?
prediction:_____   count: _____

hinge

Figure B

How many Rabbit Rays?
prediction:_____   count: _____

hinge

Figure C

How many Rabbit Rays?
prediction:_____   count: _____

hinge

Figure D

How many Rabbit Rays?
prediction:_____   count: _____

hinge

Figure E

How many Rabbit Rays?
prediction:_____   count: _____

    © 2000 AIMS Education Foundation

Rabbit Ray's Protractors

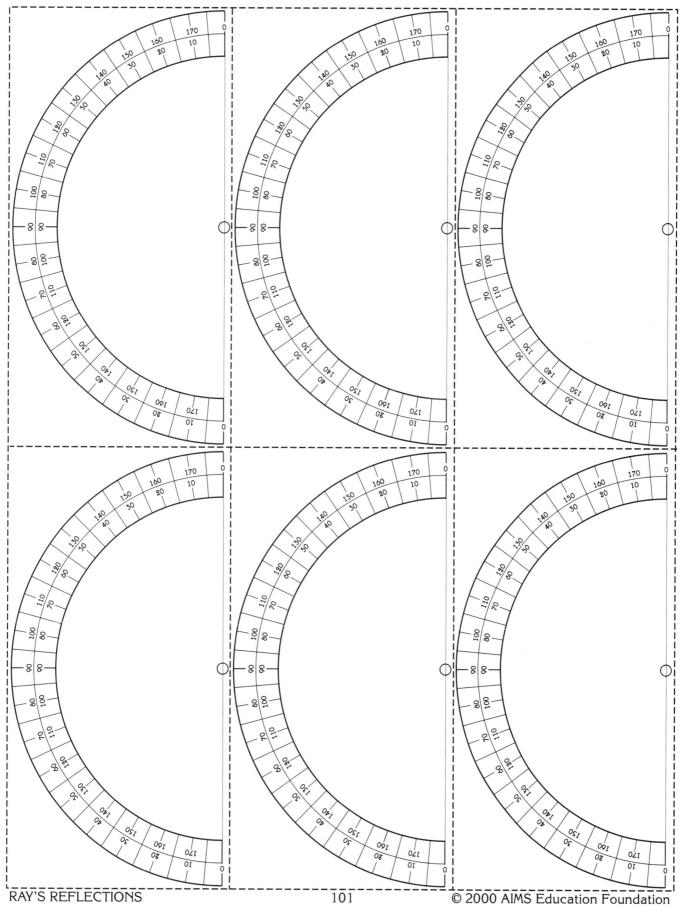

© 2000 AIMS Education Foundation

Use a protractor to measure and record the measure of the angle of the hinged mirror in figures A through E on your *Angles and Images* page.

Start each protractor measure by placing the circle on the protractor over the circle at the vertex of the angles.

Recopy in the table below the actual number of images you counted.

Angle	Angle Measure of Hinged Mirror	Actual No. of Images
Figure A		
Figure B		
Figure C		
Figure D		
Figure E		

Look for a pattern in the table and describe the relationship between the number of degrees in the angle formed by the hinged mirror and the number of images seen in the mirror.

Open and Shut

CHECK IT OUT!

To test the relationship you found between the nubmer of degrees in the angle fromed by the hinged miror and the number of images seen in the mirror, record in the table below your prediction for the number of stars you should see for each angle measure listed in the table.

Use your hinged mirror and the modified protractor to check the accuracy of your prediction. Record the actual number of stars (remember to count the printed star as an image) in the table.

Angle Measure of Hinged Mirror	Predicted No. of Star Images	Actual No. of Star Images
30°		
20°		
15°		
10°		

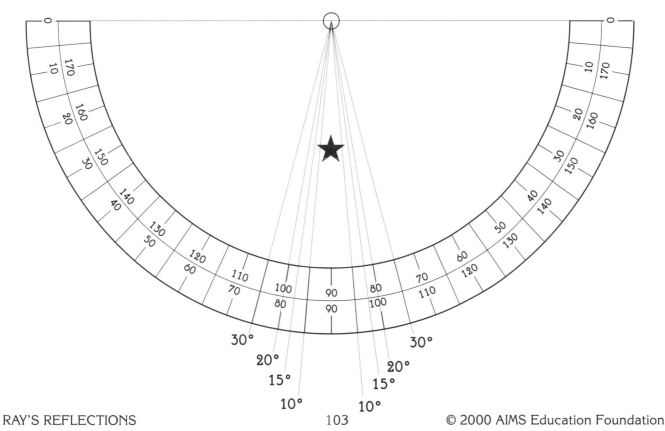

 © 2000 AIMS Education Foundation

A Line of View

Topic
Plane reflection
    multiple images

Key Question
What geometric figures can be observed if a line segment is reflected in a hinged mirror?

Focus
Students will use a hinged mirror to explore the multiple reflections of a line segment. By varying the angle between the two hinged mirrors, students will observe the formation of various geometric shapes such as a triangle, square, and hexagon.

Guiding Documents
Project 2061 Benchmark
• ...*Something can be "seen" when light waves emitted or reflected by it enter the eye...*

NRC Standards
• *Light travels in a straight line until it strikes an object. Light can be reflected by a mirror, refracted by a lens, or absorbed by the object.*
• *Light interacts with matter by transmission (including refraction), absorption, or scattering (including reflection). To see an object, light from the object—emitted by or scattered from it—must enter the eye.*

NCTM Standard 2000*
• *Recognize geometric ideas and relationships and apply them to other disciplines and to problems that arise in the classroom or in everyday life*

Math
Geometry and spatial sense
    polygon
        regular polygon
            convex polygon
            concave polygon
Science
Physical science
    plane reflection
        multiple reflections

Integrated Processes
Observing
Generalizing
Applying

Materials
Hinged mirrors

Background Information
In the *Open and Shut* activity, students observed multiple images in a hinged mirror. Some students may have also observed that the images appeared to be standing at the corners (vertices) of polygons. For example, in the diagram below, the object and its two images appear to be located at the corners of a triangle.

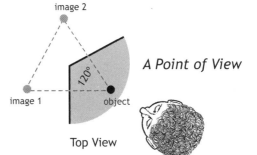

A Point of View

Top View

In this activity, instead of observing the multiple images of a point-like object (a black dot for example), students will observe what happens when a line segment replaces the point-like object.

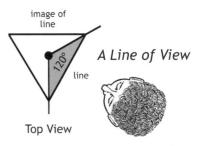

A Line of View

Top View

Multiple reflections of a line segment can produce both regular and irregular polygons. A *polygon* is a closed two-dimensional figure formed by the line segments that connect (without crossing) three or more points not in a straight line. *A regular polygon is a polygon in which all sides have equal length and all angles have equal measure.*

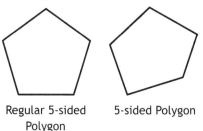

Regular 5-sided   5-sided Polygon
Polygon

Polygons can also be classified as *convex* or *concave*. A *convex polygon* is a polygon in which each interior angle is less than 180°. Any straight line through a convex polygon intersects at *most* two sides. All the diagonals of a convex polygon are contained within the polygon.

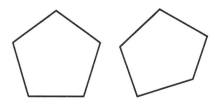

Convex, 5-sided Polygons

A *concave polygon* is a polygon in which at least one interior angle is *more* than 180°. Also, at least one straight line through a concave polygon intersects *more* than two sides. At least one diagonal is external to the polygon.

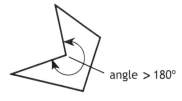

angle > 180°

Concave 5-sided Polygon

Both convex and concave polygons can be formed by reflecting a line segment in a hinged mirror.

To create regular convex polygons, place the vertex of a hinged mirror above a line so that the line crosses the bottom of each mirror at the same distance from the vertex (the sides of the mirror from the vertex to the line and the line form an isosceles triangle). Open or close each mirror the same amount.

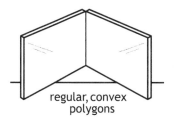

regular, convex
polygons

If only one mirror is moved, irregular convex polygons, and, eventually, concave polygons are observed.

To create concave polygons, place the vertex of the hinged mirror close to and to the side of the line.

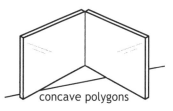

concave polygons

Move only the right-hand mirror towards the other mirror and you will observe a series of "stars."

The purpose of this activity is to introduce students to reflecting a line segment in a hinged mirror. It is left to the discretion of the teacher as to the amount of background information to share with students.

Since so much can be seen by reflecting a line segment in a hinged mirror, the following activity, *Another Line of View,* restricts investigation to regular, convex polygons. A hinged mirror can now be used to establish angle relationships for convex polygons.

Management

Organize students into groups of two and provide each group a hinged mirror.

Procedure

1. Distribute the *A Line of View* student page.
2. Instruct students to place the vertex of a hinged mirror on the dot and to open the mirrors so that the straight line printed on the page crosses the bottom of each mirror at the same distance from the vertex (the sides of the mirror from the vertex to the line and the line form an isosceles triangle).

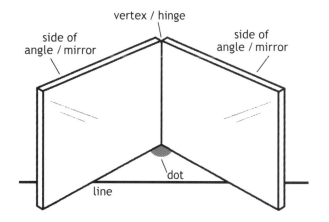

vertex / hinge

side of
angle / mirror

side of
angle / mirror

dot

line

3. Tell the students to look into the hinged mirror and open and close the hinged mirror (being sure to move each side of the hinged mirror the same amount).

 © 2000 AIMS Education Foundation

4. Have the students sketch (in the space below the line) several of the geometric shapes they discover in the hinged mirrors.
5. Distribute the *Lines of View* student page. Instruct the students to use a hinged mirror to explore the multiple-line pattern at the top of the page.
6. Point out to students the different location of the dot in the pattern at the bottom of the page. Tell students to place the vertex of the hinged mirror on the spot and then open and close the hinged mirror.
7. Distribute the *More Lines of View* student page and instruct the students to use the hinged mirror to explore the three decorated lines.

Discussion

The level of discussion following this activity is related to the amount of background information shared with students. Although students are encouraged to explore multiple line reflection, increasing their knowledge and understanding of geometry concepts and vocabulary can only add to their enjoyment of observing multiple reflections.

1. On the *A Line of View* page, describe two of the shapes you drew.
2. How are the shapes different? [different number of sides] How are they alike? [closed figures]
3. On the *Line of View* page, describe the figures you observed when you placed a hinged mirror on the top pattern (dot centered over the line pattern).
4. Again, on the *Line of View* page, describe the figures seen when you placed a hinged mirror on the line pattern at the bottom of the page (dot over right side of pattern). [The "star" patterns observed are good examples of concave polygons.]
5. On the *More Lines of View* page, describe what effect adding different colors to each pattern would have on what's seen in the hinged mirror. What science toy uses this effect? [kaleidoscope]
6. How is what you observed in this activity like what you observed in *Open and Shut*? [The smaller the angle of the mirrors, the more images (line segments) seen.]

Extensions

1. Have each student create a line design and explore its reflection in a hinged mirror. Then tell them to exchange designs.
2. Encourage students to explore their environment with a hinged mirror. For example, if a hinged mirror is placed at the corner of a book, a concave polygon-shaped hole can be observed.

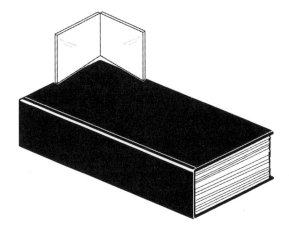

* Reprinted with permission from *Principles and Standards for School Mathematics,* 2000 by the National Council of Teachers of Mathematics. All rights reserved.

© 2000 AIMS Education Foundation

A Line of View

Name _____

Place the vertex of a hinged mirror at the dot. Keep the vertex of the mirror on the dot and open and close the hinged mirror. As you explore, sketch the geometric shapes you see in the hinged mirror in the space below the line.

●

Lines of View

Name _____

Place the vertex of a hinged mirror at the dot. Keep the vertex of the mirror on the dot and open and close the hinged mirror.

More Lines of View

Place the vertex of a hinged mirror at the dot. Keep the vertex of the mirror on the dot and open and close the hinged mirror.

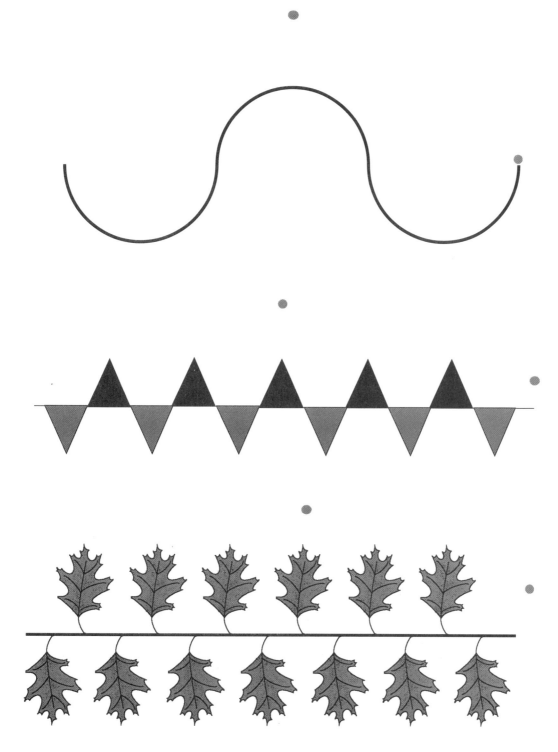

Another Line of View

Topic
Plane mirror reflection
   multiple images

Key Question
What is the relationship between the angle at the vertex of a hinged mirror and the interior and exterior angles of a regular polygon observed in the hinged mirror?

Focus
Students will use a hinged mirror to reflect a straight line segment to create the images of a series of regular polygons. They will use a protractor scale to measure the angle formed at the vertex of the hinged mirrors for each regular polygon. Students will then relate this angle to both the interior and exterior angles of the polygon.

Guiding Documents
Project 2061 Benchmark
- *...Something can be "seen" when light waves emitted or reflected by it enter the eye...*

NRC Standards
- *Light travels in a straight line until it strikes an object. Light can be reflected by a mirror, refracted by a lens, or absorbed by the object.*
- *Light interacts with matter by transmission (including refraction), absorption, or scattering (including reflection). To see an object, light from the object—emitted by or scattered from it—must enter the eye.*

NCTM Standards 2000*
- *Recognize geometric ideas and relationships and apply them to other disciplines and to problems that arise in the classroom or in everyday life*
- *Understand such attributes as length, area, weight, volume, and size of angle and select the appropriate type of unit for measuring each attribute*
- *Use geometric models to solve problems in other areas of mathematics, such as number and measurement*

Math
Geometry and spatial sense
   regular polygon
      interior, exterior angle
      angle sum of a straight line

Science
Physical science
   plane reflection
      multiple images of a line

Integrated Processes
Observing
Comparing and contrasting
Generalizing

Materials
Hinged mirrors
Rulers
Protractors

Background Information
A *regular polygon* is a polygon in which all sides have equal length and all angles have equal measure. For example, a regular octagon is shown in this figure.

8 sided regular octagon

An *interior angle* of a polygon is formed between two sides with the same vertex (adjacent sides).

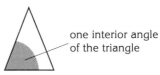

one interior angle
of the triangle

An *exterior angle* of a polygon is formed whenever one of its sides is *extended through* a vertex.

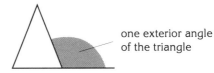

one exterior angle
of the triangle

For any polygon, the sum of the interior angle and exterior angle formed at the same vertex is 180°.

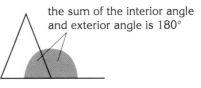

the sum of the interior angle
and exterior angle is 180°

Management
1. If protractors are not available, make transparencies of the *Rabbit Ray's Protractors* page.
2. The polygons that appear on the student pages are purposely drawn large to facilitate measuring the interior and exterior angles.

Procedure

1. Distribute the rulers, protractors, and the *Interior and Exterior Angles* pages.
2. Use the diagrams at the top of the student page to review the definitions of interior and exterior angle with the students.
3. Instruct the students to shade and label one interior angle in each of the five polygons.
4. Have the students use a ruler to extend one of the sides that forms the shaded interior angle of each polygon. Tell them to shade and label the exterior angle.
5. Tell the students to use a protractor to measure and record the interior and exterior angle for each polygon.
6. Distribute hinged mirrors and the *Angle Relationships* student page.
7. Instruct the students to transfer the data from the *Interior and Exterior Angles* pages to the *Angle Relationships* page.
8. Tell the students to place the vertex of the hinged mirror on the shaded dot and to use the guidelines to adjust both sides of the hinged mirror until a triangle is observed. Instruct the students to use the protractor scale (each division = 5°) to measure and record the angle at the vertex of the hinged mirror.
9. Repeat step eight for the four remaining polygons.
10. Tell the students to compute and record the sum of the interior and exterior angle for each polygon.

Discussion

1. Compare your interior-exterior angle data with the data in the table.

Regular Polygon	# of degrees in one interior angle	# of degrees in one exterior angle
triangle	60°	120°
square	90°	90°
pentagon	108°	72°
hexagon	120°	60°
octagon	135°	45°

2. What patterns do you notice in the table?
3. Compare the data you recorded with the data in the table.

Regular Polygon	# of sides	angle measure of hinged mirror	angle mesaure of one interior angle	angle mesaure of one exterior angle	sum of interior and exterior angles
triangle	3	120°	60°	120°	180°
square	4	90°	90°	90°	180°
pentagon	5	72°	108°	72°	180°
hexagon	6	60°	120°	60°	180°
octagon	8	45°	135°	45°	180°

4. How are the interior and exterior angles for each regular polygon related? [The sum of the interior and exterior angles equals 180°.]
5. How is the angle of the hinged mirror related to the exterior angle of each regular polygon? [The angles are equal.]
6. How is the angle of the hinged mirror related to the interior angle of each regular polygon? [The angle at the vertex of the hinged mirror equals 180° minus the measure of the interior angle.]
7. The interior angle of a regular ten-sided polygon, called a dodecagon, is 144°. How would you compute the interior angle? [180° – 144° = 36°] Use your hinged mirror to verify your computation.

Extension

The Logo (turtle geometry) computer programming language was developed specifically for educational use and makes extensive use of the interior-exterior angle concept.

The Logo "turtle" can be commanded to move forward, turn right, and turn left. As the turtle moves, it leaves a trail. A beginning Logo exercise asks the student to write a program that has the turtle draw an equilateral triangle.

Assume the length of one side of the triangle is 100 turtle steps. The command *forward 100* moves the turtle 100 steps from point A to point B. At point B, the command *right 120* causes the turtle to turn right 120°, through the exterior angle. Another *forward 100* moves the turtle to point C. The turtle turns another 120° to the right and moves 100 steps to return to point A to complete the triangle.

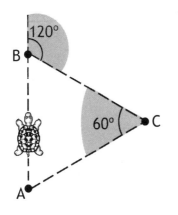

The nested set of regular polygons shown in the following figure was created by the one-line Logo programming procedure named gpoly. Gpoly stands for generalized polygon procedure.

```
to gpoly :size :side
  repeat :side [fd :size rt 360/:side]
end
```

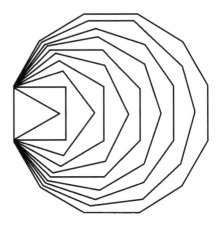

Beginners will often try to use the 60° interior angle to program the turtle to draw an equilateral triangle.

These steps are combined into one procedure (shown below) named *triangle*. Now, anytime the word "triangle" is typed into the computer, the turtle draws an equilateral triangle.

```
to triangle
  forward 100 right 120
  forward 100 right 120
  forward 100 right 120
end
```

Free Windows® and Macintosh® versions of the Logo programming language can be downloaded from the following web site:
www.media.mit.edu/groups/logo-foundation

*   Reprinted with permission from *Principles and Standards for School Mathematics*, 2000 by the National Council of Teachers of Mathematics. All rights reserved.

Rabbit Ray's Protractors

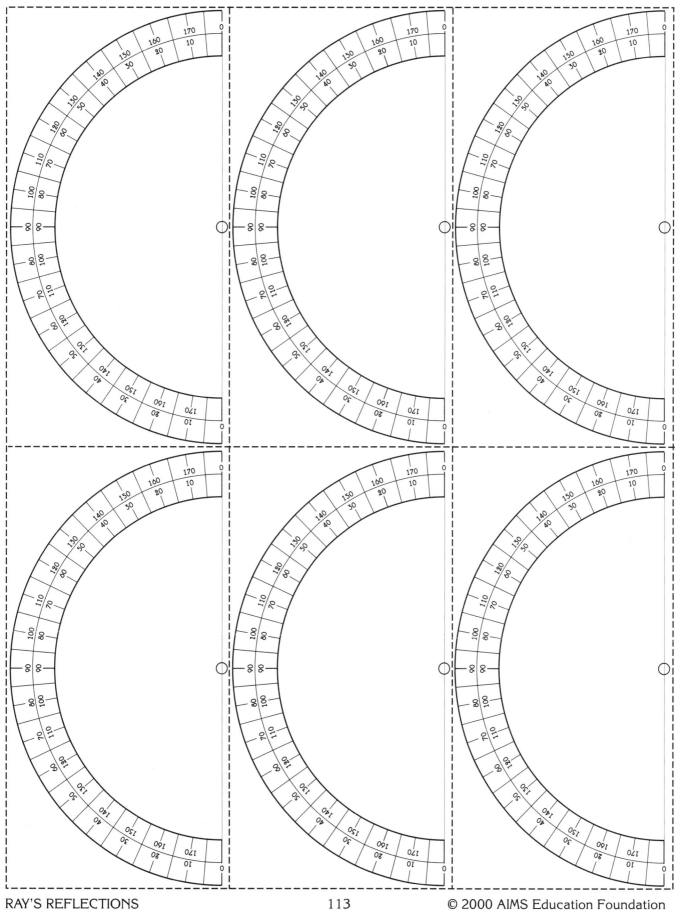

Another Line of View

Interior and Exterior Angles

Name _____

An interior angle of a polygon is formed between two sides with the same vertex (adjacent sides).

one interior angle of the triangle is labeled "I"

An exterior angle of a polygon is formed whenever one of its sides is extended through a vertex.

one exterior angle of the triangle is labeled "E"

1. Shade and label one interior angle in each of the five polygons.
2. For each of the five polygons, shade and label the exterior angle formed by extending one of the sides that contains the shaded interior angle.
3. Use your protractor to measure and record the interior and exterior angle for each polygon.

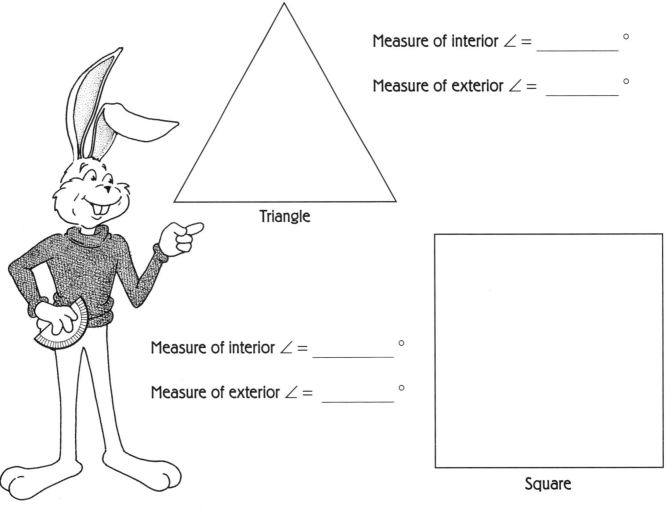

Measure of interior ∠ = _____ °

Measure of exterior ∠ = _____ °

Triangle

Measure of interior ∠ = _____ °

Measure of exterior ∠ = _____ °

Square

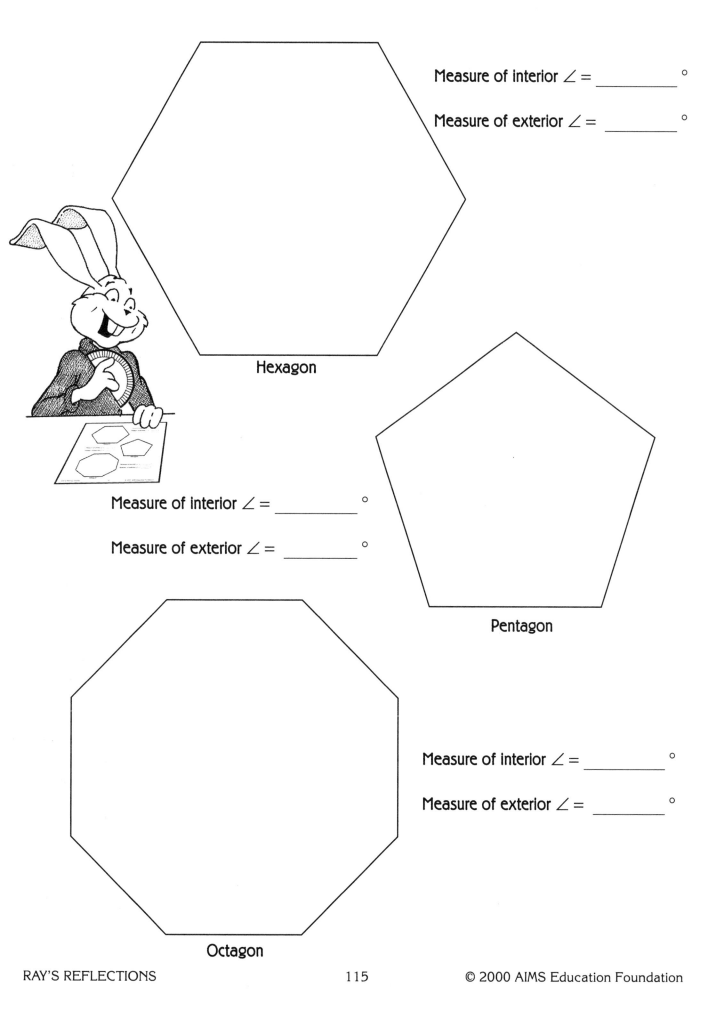

Measure of interior ∠ = _____ °

Measure of exterior ∠ = _____ °

Hexagon

Measure of interior ∠ = _____ °

Measure of exterior ∠ = _____ °

Pentagon

Measure of interior ∠ = _____ °

Measure of exterior ∠ = _____ °

Octagon

 © 2000 AIMS Education Foundation

Another Line of View
Angle Relationships

Use a hinged mirror and your angle measure data to complete the following chart.

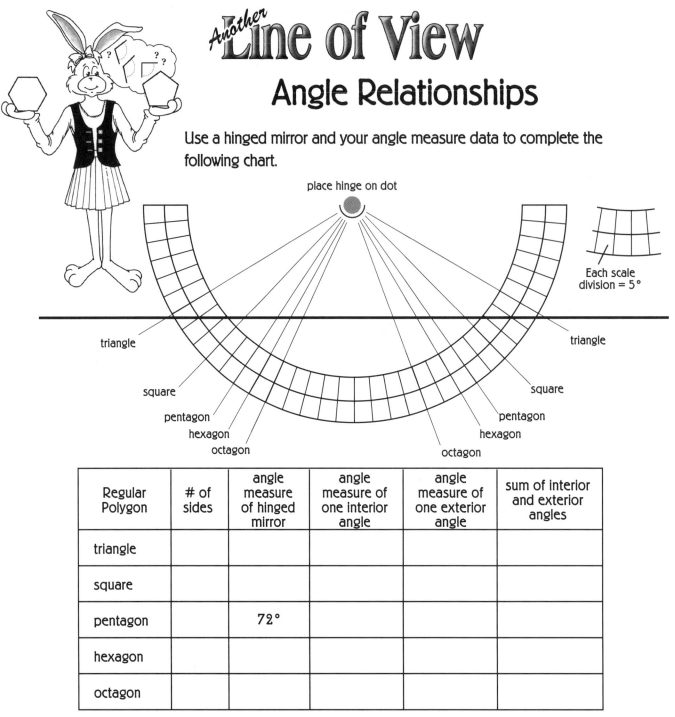

place hinge on dot

Each scale division = 5°

triangle · square · pentagon · hexagon · octagon

triangle · square · pentagon · hexagon · octagon

Regular Polygon	# of sides	angle measure of hinged mirror	angle measure of one interior angle	angle measure of one exterior angle	sum of interior and exterior angles
triangle					
square					
pentagon		72°			
hexagon					
octagon					

1. How are the interior and exterior angles related for each regular polygon?

2. How is the angle of the hinged mirror related to the exterior angle of each regular polygon?

3. How is the angle of the hinged mirror related to the interior angle of each regular polygon?

Topic
Mirror symmetry

Key Questions
What can we discover about the symmetry of letters of the alphabet by using a mirror?

Focus
Students will explore how a plane mirror reflects letters when placed inside and outside of the letter. Students will use a Venn diagram to record and analyze data.

Guiding Documents
Project 2061 Benchmark
- *Symmetry can be found by reflection, turns, or slides.*

NCTM Standards 2000*
- *Recognize geometric ideas and relationships and apply them to other disciplines and to problems that arise in the classroom or in everyday life*
- *Identify and describe line and rotational symmetry in two- and three-dimensional shapes and designs*
- *Collect data using observations, surveys, and experiments*

Math
Geometry and spatial sense
   line symmetry

Science
Physical science
   light
      plane reflection

Integrated Processes
Observing
Collecting and recording data
Comparing and contrasting
Generalizing

Materials
For each pair of students:
   plane mirror and support stand

Background Information
Symmetry with Respect to a Line
   Two points are symmetric with respect to a line if, *and only if*, that line perpendicularly bisects the line segment

joining the two points. In the diagram, points *A* and *C* are symmetric with respect to line *L*. Line *L* is the perpendicular bisector of line segment connecting point *A* and point *B*.

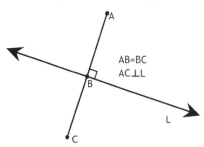

   A geometric figure is symmetric with respect to a line if, and only if, every point on the figure on one side of the line is matched by a symmetrical point on the opposite side of the line of symmetry.

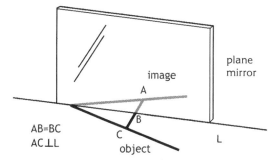

   When letters of the alphabet are reflected in a plane mirror placed on the letter, some will appear in the mirror exactly as they are written on paper and others will appear backwards or upside down. The reason for this is that some letters have lines of symmetry and others do not. For example, the upper case A has a line of symmetry but the upper case G does not.

   Letter symmetry is first explored in this activity by having students stand the mirror on the letter and attempt to find a line of symmetry. This inside line of symmetry may be a horizontal or vertical line or, for some letters, there may not be an inside line of symmetry. Some letters may have both a horizontal and a vertical line of symmetry. A pencil line drawn along the bottom of the mirror establishes this line of symmetry. Following are examples of a vertical line of symmetry, a horizontal line of symmetry, both lines of symmetry, and no line of symmetry.

Lines of Symmetry Inside a Letter

vertical line
of symmetry

horizontal line
of symmetry

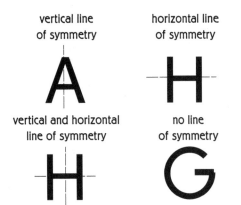

vertical and horizontal
line of symmetry

no line
of symmetry

In the second half of this activity, students will explore horizontal and vertical line symmetry by placing a mirror to the right of the letter or above the letter. If the letter matches exactly its reflection, it is symmetric with respect to the outside line.

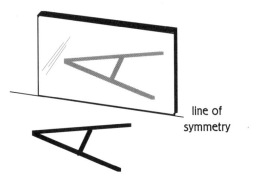

line of
symmetry

A pencil line drawn along the bottom of the mirror establishes this line of symmetry. Following are examples.

Lines of Symmetry Outside a Letter
that Reflect the Letter Unchanged

vertical line of symmetry

horizontal line of symmetry

mirror image

mirror image

vertical and horizontal
line of symmetry

no
reflecting
line

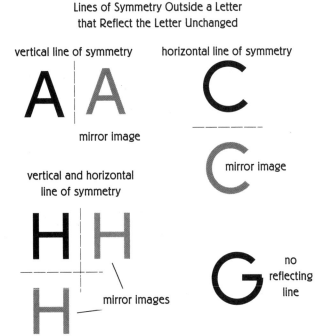

mirror images

A *Venn* diagram is made up of geometric figures that picture sets and set relationships.

For example, let U, the universal set, equal the set of *Whole Numbers*. In set notation, U = {0, 1, 2, 3, 4, ...}.

Let set A = {1, 2, 4, 6, 8} and set B = {0, 4, 8, 12}.

The following Venn diagram represents the relationships between the universal set, set A, and set B. The region of the diagram labeled A ∩ B is called the *intersection* of set A and set B. It is the set of elements common to *both A and B*.

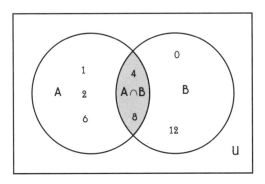

In the activity, students will use Venn diagrams to identify those letters that have horizontal, vertical, both horizontal and vertical lines of symmetry, and no line of symmetry.

A comparison of the completed Venn diagrams, one for lines inside the letter and one for outside lines, will show that they are the same. In other words, for a letter to have a line outside of the letter that reflects it unchanged, the letter must have an inside line of symmetry.

One way to think about this requirement is to consider the reflection of the double-colored letter in the following diagram.

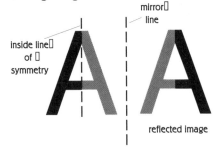

mirror
line

inside line
of
symmetry

reflected image

The inside line of symmetry for the letter on the left is shown. If a mirror is placed on the mirror line in the diagram, the left, black half of the letter will be reflected to form the right-half of the reflected image. The right half of the letter on the left will be reflected to form the left half of the reflected image. The fact that letters are typically a solid color hides this fact.

Management

1. Students may share mirrors if one cannot be provided for each student.
2. Teach or review the properties of a Venn diagram.

Procedure

1. Distribute the *Mirror Twins Alphabet* page.
2. Distribute the *Inside Lines of Symmetry* page.
3. Use the large letters at the top of the *Inside Lines of Symmetry* page to show students how to use a mirror to find lines of symmetry. Instruct the students to test each letter on the *Mirror Twins Alphabet* page as to whether it has one, two, or no lines of symmetry. Tell them to record the result of each test in the proper section of the Venn diagram.
4. Distribute the *Outside Lines of Symmetry* page.
5. Use the large letters at the top of the *Outside Lines of Symmetry* page to show students how to use a mirror to find lines of symmetry that leave the reflected letter unchanged. Instruct the students to test each letter on the *Mirror Twins Alphabet* page as to whether it has one, two, or no outside lines of symmetry. Tell them to record the result of each test in the proper section of the Venn diagram.

Discussion

1. What letters of the alphabet have either a vertical or horizontal line of symmetry?
2. What letters have both?
3. What letters don't have a line of symmetry?
4. Compare your Venn diagram with the following diagram.

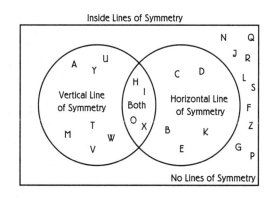

Inside Lines of Symmetry

5. What letters have a reflecting line to the side of the letter that reflects the letter so that it appears unchanged?
6. What letters have a reflecting line above the letter that reflects the letter so that it appears unchanged?
7. What letters do not have an outside reflecting line?
8. Compare your Venn diagram with the following diagram.

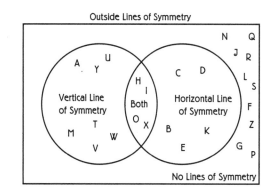

Outside Lines of Symmetry

9. Compare the two Venn diagrams.
10. If you were going to compile a list of words that looks exactly like their mirror reflection, MOM, for example, how would you select the letters?
11. Why is

AMBULANCE

painted on the front of an ambulance? [Drivers in front of an ambulance, when hearing the ambulance's siren and seeing its flashing lights, naturally look into the rear-view mirror and see the word AMBULANCE. For this to happen, the sign painted on the front of the ambulance has to be reversed.]
12. Besides letters, for what other things could you use a mirror to find a line of symmetry?

Extensions

1. Have students compile a list of words that are exactly like their mirror reflection. [BEE, HIKE, MOM, BOX, BIKE, HIDE, KID, DICE, ICE, etc. is only a partial list of possible words.]
2. Have students write "secret" messages by writing only half of the letter that is symmetrical. For example,

（I DID MY MATH.)

3. Have the students assign the following values to the sections of one of the Venn diagrams.

no line of symmetry	0 points
1 line of symmetry	1 point
2 lines of symmetry	2 points

Ask each student to compute the "value" of their full name and then to compare their scores with their classmates.

*   Reprinted with permission from *Principles and Standards for School Mathematics,* 2000 by the National Council of Teachers of Mathematics. All rights reserved.

MIRROR TWINS
Alphabet

A B C D E

F G H I J K

L M N O P

Q R S T U

V W X Y Z

 © 2000 AIMS Education Foundation

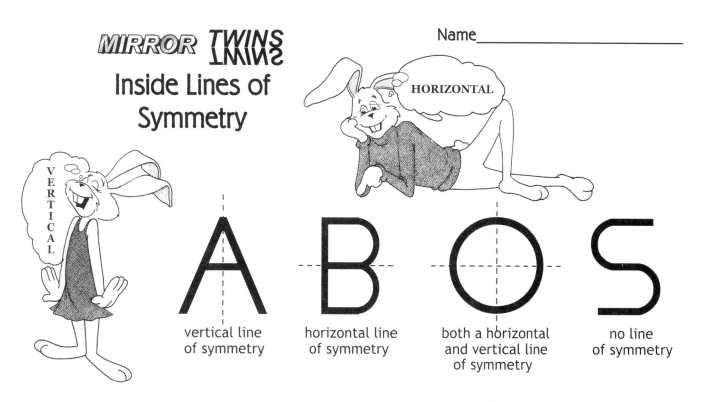

MIRROR TWINS

Inside Lines of
Symmetry

HORIZONTAL

VERTICAL

A   B   O   S

vertical line
of symmetry

horizontal line
of symmetry

both a horizontal
and vertical line
of symmetry

no line
of symmetry

Stand a mirror "inside" each letter and determine if the letter has either a horizontal or vertical line of symmetry. If there is a vertical or horizontal line of symmetry for that letter, record that letter in the correct section of the Venn diagram.

Some letters may not have a line of symmetry. Record those letters in the correct section of the Venn diagram.

Other letters may have both a horizontal and vertical line of symmetry. Review your Venn diagram and move any letters that have both a vertical and horizontal line of symmetry to the Both section of the diagram.

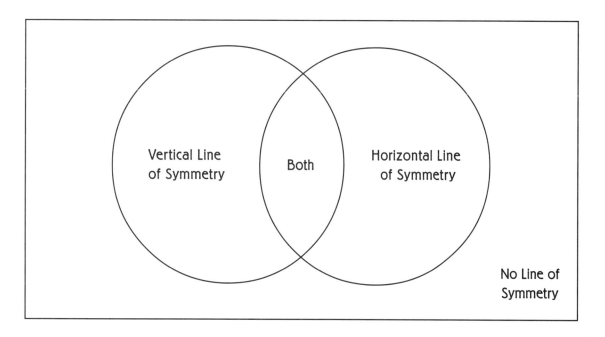

Vertical Line
of Symmetry

Both

Horizontal Line
of Symmetry

No Line of
Symmetry

Name_____

Outside Lines of Symmetry

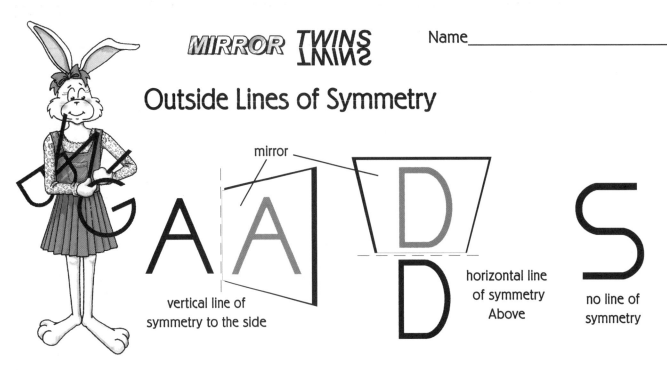

mirror

vertical line of symmetry to the side

horizontal line of symmetry Above

no line of symmetry

Stand a mirror to the right side of each letter on the Alphabet page and determine if there is a vertical line of symmetry for that letter. If so, record that letter in the Venn diagram.

Stand a mirror above each letter on the Alphabet page and determine if there is a horizontal line of symmetry for that letter. If so, record that letter in the Venn diagram.

Some letters may not have a line of symmetry. Record those letters in the Venn diagram.

Other letters may have both a horizontal and vertical line of symmetry. Review your Venn diagram and move any letters that have both a vertical and horizontal line of symmetry to the Both section of the diagram.

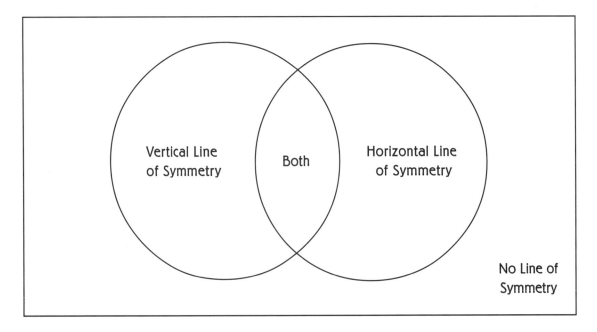

Vertical Line of Symmetry   Both   Horizontal Line of Symmetry

No Line of Symmetry

The AIMS Program

AIMS is the acronym for "**A**ctivities **I**ntegrating **M**athematics and **S**cience." Such integration enriches learning and makes it meaningful and holistic. AIMS began as a project of Fresno Pacific University to integrate the study of mathematics and science in grades K-9, but has since expanded to include language arts, social studies, and other disciplines.

AIMS is a continuing program of the non-profit AIMS Education Foundation. It had its inception in a National Science Foundation funded program whose purpose was to explore the effectiveness of integrating mathematics and science. The project directors in cooperation with 80 elementary classroom teachers devoted two years to a thorough field-testing of the results and implications of integration.

The approach met with such positive results that the decision was made to launch a program to create instructional materials incorporating this concept. Despite the fact that thoughtful educators have long recommended an integrative approach, very little appropriate material was available in 1981 when the project began. A series of writing projects have ensued and today the AIMS Education Foundation is committed to continue the creation of new integrated activities on a permanent basis.

The AIMS program is funded through the sale of this developing series of books and proceeds from the Foundation's endowment. All net income from program and products flows into a trust fund administered by the AIMS Education Foundation. Use of these funds is restricted to support of research, development, and publication of new materials. Writers donate all their rights to the Foundation to support its on-going program. No royalties are paid to the writers.

The rationale for integration lies in the fact that science, mathematics, language arts, social studies, etc., are integrally interwoven in the real world from which it follows that they should be similarly treated in the classroom where we are preparing students to live in that world. Teachers who use the AIMS program give enthusiastic endorsement to the effectiveness of this approach.

Science encompasses the art of questioning, investigating, hypothesizing, discovering, and communicating. Mathematics is a language that provides clarity, objectivity, and understanding. The language arts provide us powerful tools of communication. Many of the major contemporary societal issues stem from advancements in science and must be studied in the context of the social sciences. Therefore, it is timely that all of us take seriously a more holistic mode of educating our students. This goal motivates all who are associated with the AIMS Program. We invite you to join us in this effort.

Meaningful integration of knowledge is a major recommendation coming from the nation's professional science and mathematics associations. The American Association for the Advancement of Science in *Science for All Americans* strongly recommends the integration of mathematics, science, and technology. The National Council of Teachers of Mathematics places strong emphasis on applications of mathematics such as are found in science investigations. AIMS is fully aligned with these recommendations.

Extensive field testing of AIMS investigations confirms these beneficial results.

1. Mathematics becomes more meaningful, hence more useful, when it is applied to situations that interest students.
2. The extent to which science is studied and understood is increased, with a significant economy of time, when mathematics and science are integrated.
3. There is improved quality of learning and retention, supporting the thesis that learning which is meaningful and relevant is more effective.
4. Motivation and involvement are increased dramatically as students investigate real-world situations and participate actively in the process.

We invite you to become part of this classroom teacher movement by using an integrated approach to learning and sharing any suggestions you may have. The AIMS Program welcomes you!

© 2000 AIMS Education Foundation

AIMS Program Publications

GRADES K-4 SERIES

Bats Incredible!
Brinca de Alegria Hacia la Primavera con las Matemáticas y Ciencias
Cáete de Gusto Hacia el Otoño con la Matemáticas y Ciencias
Cycles of Knowing and Growing
Fall Into Math and Science
Field Detectives
Glide Into Winter With Math and Science
Hardhatting in a Geo-World (Revised Edition, 1996)
Jaw Breakers and Heart Thumpers (Revised Edition, 1995)
Los Cincos Sentidos
Overhead and Underfoot (Revised Edition, 1994)
Patine al Invierno con Matemáticas y Ciencias
Popping With Power (Revised Edition, 1996)
Primariamente Física (Revised Edition, 1994)
Primarily Earth
Primariamente Plantas
Primarily Physics (Revised Edition, 1994)
Primarily Plants
Sense-able Science
Spring Into Math and Science
Under Construction

GRADES K-6 SERIES

Budding Botanist
Critters
El Botanista Principiante
Exploring Environments
Fabulous Fractions
Mostly Magnets
Ositos Nada Más
Primarily Bears
Principalmente Imanes
Water Precious Water

GRADES 5-9 SERIES

Actions with Fractions
Brick Layers
Brick Layers II
Conexiones Eléctricas
Down to Earth
Electrical Connections
Finding Your Bearings (Revised Edition, 1996)
Floaters and Sinkers (Revised Edition, 1995)
From Head to Toe
Fun With Foods
Gravity Rules!
Historical Connections in Mathematics, Volume I
Historical Connections in Mathematics, Volume II
Historical Connections in Mathematics, Volume III
Just for the Fun of It!
Machine Shop
Magnificent Microworld Adventures
Math + Science, A Solution
Off the Wall Science: A Poster Series Revisited
Our Wonderful World
Out of This World (Revised Edition, 1994)
Pieces and Patterns, A Patchwork in Math and Science
Piezas y Diseños, un Mosaic de Matemáticas y Ciencias
Proportional Reasoning
Ray's Reflections
Soap Films and Bubbles
Spatial Visualization
The Sky's the Limit (Revised Edition, 1994)
The Amazing Circle, Volume 1
Through the Eyes of the Explorers:
   Minds-on Math & Mapping
What's Next, Volume 1
What's Next, Volume 2
What's Next, Volume 3

For further information write to:
AIMS Education Foundation • P.O. Box 8120 • Fresno, California 93747-8120
www.AIMSedu.org/ • Fax 559•255•6396

© 2000 AIMS Education Foundation

AIMS Education Foundation Programs

A Day with AIMS

Intensive one-day workshops are offered to introduce educators to the philosophy and rationale of AIMS. Participants will discuss the methodology of AIMS and the strategies by which AIMS principles may be incorporated into curriculum. Each participant will take part in a variety of hands-on AIMS investigations to gain an understanding of such aspects as the scientific/mathematical content, classroom management, and connections with other curricular areas. *A Day with AIMS* workshops may be offered anywhere in the United States. Necessary supplies and take-home materials are usually included in the enrollment fee.

A Week with AIMS

Throughout the nation, AIMS offers many one-week workshops each year, usually in the summer. Each workshop lasts five days and includes at least 30 hours of AIMS hands-on instruction. Participants are grouped according to the grade level(s) in which they are interested. Instructors are members of the AIMS Instructional Leadership Network. Supplies for the activities and a generous supply of take-home materials are included in the enrollment fee. Sites are selected on the basis of applications submitted by educational organizations. If chosen to host a workshop, the host agency agrees to provide specified facilities and cooperate in the promotion of the workshop. The AIMS Education Foundation supplies workshop materials as well as the travel, housing, and meals for instructors.

AIMS One-Week Perspectives Workshops

Each summer, Fresno Pacific University offers AIMS one-week workshops on its campus in Fresno, California. AIMS Program Directors and highly qualified members of the AIMS National Leadership Network serve as instructors.

The Science Festival and the Festival of Mathematics

Each summer, Fresno Pacific University offers a Science Festival and a Festival of Mathematics. These festivals have gained national recognition as inspiring and challenging experiences, giving unique opportunities to experience hands-on mathematics and science in topical and grade-level groups. Guest faculty includes some of the nation's most highly regarded mathematics and science educators. Supplies and take-home materials are included in the enrollment fee.

The AIMS Instructional Leadership Program

This is an AIMS staff-development program seeking to prepare facilitators for leadership roles in science/math education in their home districts or regions. Upon successful completion of the program, trained facilitators may become members of the AIMS Instructional Leadership Network, qualified to conduct AIMS workshops, teach AIMS in-service courses for college credit, and serve as AIMS consultants. Intensive training is provided in mathematics, science, process and thinking skills, workshop management, and other relevant topics.

College Credit and Grants

Those who participate in workshops may often qualify for college credit. If the workshop takes place on the campus of Fresno Pacific University, that institution may grant appropriate credit. If the workshop takes place off-campus, arrangements can sometimes be made for credit to be granted by another institution. In addition, the applicant's home school district is often willing to grant in-service or professional-development credit. Many educators who participate in AIMS workshops are recipients of various types of educational grants, either local or national. Nationally known foundations and funding agencies have long recognized the value of AIMS mathematics and science workshops to educators. The AIMS Education Foundation encourages educators interested in attending or hosting workshops to explore the possibilities suggested above. Although the Foundation strongly supports such interest, it reminds applicants that they have the primary responsibility for fulfilling *current* requirements.

For current information regarding the programs described above, please complete the following:

Information Request

Please send current information on the items checked:

___ *Basic Information Packet* on AIMS materials
___ *AIMS Instructional Leadership Program*
___ *AIMS One-Week Perspectives* workshops

___ *A Week with AIMS* workshops
___ Hosting information for *A Day with AIMS* workshops
___ Hosting information for *A Week with AIMS* workshops

Name _____ Phone _____

Address _____

Street	City	State	Zip

We invite you to subscribe to AIMS!

Each issue of *AIMS* contains a variety of material useful to educators at all grade levels. Feature articles of lasting value deal with topics such as mathematical or science concepts, curriculum, assessment, the teaching of process skills, and historical background. Several of the latest AIMS math/science investigations are always included, along with their reproducible activity sheets. As needs direct and space allows, various issues contain news of current developments, such as workshop schedules, activities of the AIMS Instructional Leadership Network, and announcements of upcoming publications.

AIMS is published monthly, August through May. Subscriptions are on an annual basis only. A subscription entered at any time will begin with the next issue, but will also include the previous issues of that volume. Readers have preferred this arrangement because articles and activities within an annual volume are often interrelated.

Please note that an *AIMS* subscription automatically includes duplication rights for one school site for all issues included in the subscription. Many schools build cost-effective library resources with their subscriptions.

YES! I am interested in subscribing to AIMS.

Name _____   Home Phone _____

Address _____   City, State, Zip _____

Please send the following volumes (subject to availability):

_____	Volume VI	(1991-92)	$30.00	_____	Volume XI	(1996-97)	$30.00

_____ Volume VI   (1991-92) $30.00   _____ Volume XI   (1996-97) $30.00

_____ Volume VII   (1992-93) $30.00   _____ Volume XII   (1997-98) $30.00

_____ Volume VIII   (1993-94) $30.00   _____ Volume XIII   (1998-99) $30.00

_____ Volume IX   (1994-95) $30.00   _____ Volume XIV   (1999-00) $30.00

_____ Volume X   (1995-96) $30.00   _____ Volume XV   (2000-01) $30.00

_____ **Limited offer: Volumes XIV & XV (1999-2001) $55.00**
    (Note: Prices may change without notice)

Check your method of payment:

❐ Check enclosed in the amount of $ _____

❐ Purchase order attached (Please include the P.O.#, the authorizing signature, and position of the authorizing person.)

❐ Credit Card   ❐ Visa   ❐ MasterCard   Amount $ _____

   Card # _____   Expiration Date _____

   Signature _____   Today's Date _____

Make checks payable to **AIMS Education Foundation**.
Mail to *AIMS* Magazine, P.O. Box 8120, Fresno, CA 93747-8120.
Phone (559) 255-4094 or (888) 733-2467   FAX (559) 255-6396
AIMS Homepage: http://www.AIMSedu.org/

© 2000 AIMS Education Foundatio

AIMS Duplication Rights Program

AIMS has received many requests from school districts for the purchase of unlimited duplication rights to AIMS materials. In response, the AIMS Education Foundation has formulated the program outlined below. There is a built-in flexibility which, we trust, will provide for those who use AIMS materials extensively to purchase such rights for either individual activities or entire books.

It is the goal of the AIMS Education Foundation to make its materials and programs available at reasonable cost. All income from the sale of publications and duplication rights is used to support AIMS programs; hence, strict adherence to regulations governing duplication is essential. Duplication of AIMS materials beyond limits set by copyright laws and those specified below is strictly forbidden.

Limited Duplication Rights

Any purchaser of an AIMS book may make up to *200 copies* of any activity in that book for use at *one school site*. Beyond that, rights must be purchased according to the appropriate category.

Unlimited Duplication Rights for Single Activities

An individual or school may purchase the right to make an unlimited number of copies of a single activity. The royalty is $5.00 per activity per school site.

Examples: 3 activities x 1 site x $5.00 = $15.00
9 activities x 3 sites x $5.00 = $135.00

Unlimited Duplication Rights for Entire Books

A school or district may purchase the right to make an unlimited number of copies of a single, *specified* book. The royalty is $20.00 per book per school site. This is in addition to the cost of the book.

Examples: 5 books x 1 site   x $20.00 = $100.00
12 books x 10 sites x $20.00 = $2400.00

Magazine/Newsletter Duplication Rights

Those who purchase *AIMS* (magazine)/*Newsletter* are hereby granted permission to make up to 200 copies of any portion of it, provided these copies will be used for educational purposes.

Workshop Instructors' Duplication Rights

Workshop instructors may distribute to registered workshop participants a maximum of 100 copies of any article and/or 100 copies of no more than eight activities, provided these six conditions are met:

1. Since all AIMS activities are based upon the *AIMS Model of Mathematics* and the *AIMS Model of Learning*, leaders must include in their presentations an explanation of these two models.
2. Workshop instructors must relate the AIMS activities presented to these basic explanations of the AIMS philosophy of education.
3. The copyright notice must appear on all materials distributed.
4. Instructors must provide information enabling participants to order books and magazines from the Foundation.
5. Instructors must inform participants of their limited duplication rights as outlined below.
6. Only student pages may be duplicated.

Written permission must be obtained for duplication beyond the limits listed above. Additional royalty payments may be required.

Workshop Participants' Rights

Those enrolled in workshops in which AIMS student activity sheets are distributed may duplicate a maximum of 35 copies or enough to use the lessons one time with one class, whichever is less. Beyond that, rights must be purchased according to the appropriate category.

Application for Duplication Rights

The purchasing agency or individual must clearly specify the following:
1. Name, address, and telephone number
2. Titles of the books for Unlimited Duplication Rights contracts
3. Titles of activities for Unlimited Duplication Rights contracts
4. Names and addresses of school sites for which duplication rights are being purchased.

NOTE: Books to be duplicated must be purchased separately and are not included in the contract for Unlimited Duplication Rights.

The requested duplication rights are automatically authorized when proper payment is received, although a *Certificate of Duplication Rights* will be issued when the application is processed.

Address all correspondence to: **Contract Division**
AIMS Education Foundation
P.O. Box 8120
Fresno, CA 93747-8120

www.AIMSedu.org/
Fax 559•255•6396

© 2000 AIMS Education Foundation

Flagler College Library
P.O. Box 1027
St. Augustine, FL 32085